Study Guide

to Accompany

Macroeconomics

Theories, Policies, and International Applications

Roger LeRoy Miller

Institute for University Studies
Arlingtion, Texas

David VanHoose

Department of Economics
Baylor University

Prepared by
David VanHoose

Australia · Canada · Mexico · Singapore · Spain · United Kingdom · United States

Study Guide

to Accompany **Macroeconomics:** Theories, Policies, and International Applications, Third Edition
by Roger LeRoy Miller, David VanHoose

Prepared by
David VanHoose, Department of Economics, Baylor University

Editorial Director Jack Calhoun	Acquisitions Editor: Michael W. Worls	Production Editor: Anne Sheroff
Vice President/Editor-in-Chief: Michael P. Roche	Senior Developmental Editor: Jan Lamar	Manufacturing Coordinator: Sandee Milewski
Publisher of Economics Michael B. Mercier	Executive Marketing Manager: Lisa L. Lysne	Printer: Globus

COPYRIGHT © 2004
by South-Western, a division of
Thomson Learning.
Thomson Learning^{TM} is a trademark
used herein under license.

ISBN: 0-324-16375-4
Printed in the United States of
America
1 2 3 4 5 06 05 04 03 02

For more information contact
South-Western,
5191 Natorp Boulevard,
Mason, Ohio 45040.
Or you can visit our Internet site at:
http://www.swlearning.com

ALL RIGHTS RESERVED.
No part of this work covered by the
copyright hereon may be reproduced
or used in any form or by any
means—graphic, electronic, or mechanical, including photocopying, recording,
taping, Web distribution or information
storage and retrieval systems—without
the written permission of the publisher.

For permission to use material from
this text or product, contact us by
Tel (800) 730-2214
Fax (800) 730-2215
http://www.thomsonrights.com

Contents

Preface v

Chapter 1
The Macroeconomy 1

Chapter 2
*How Do We Know How We're Doing? —
Measuring Macroeconomic Variables* 9

Chapter 3
*The Self-Adjusting Economy — Classical Macroeconomic Theory:
Employment, Output, and Prices* 21

Chapter 4
*Classical Macroeconomic Theory —
Interest Rates and Exchange Rates* 30

Chapter 5
*Utopia Just Beyond the Horizon, or Future Shock? —
The Theory of Economic Growth* 38

Chapter 6
*Business Cycles and Short-Run Macroeconomics —
Essentials of the Keynesian System* 48

Chapter 7
*A Meaningful Role for Government —
Fiscal Policy in the Traditional Keynesian System* 61

Chapter 8
*Do Central Banks Matter? —
Money in the Traditional Keynesian System* 71

Chapter 9
*The Open Economy —
Exchange Rates and the Balance of Payments* 85

Chapter 10
Is There a Trade-off Between Unemployment and Inflation? —
The Keynesian and Monetarist Views on Price and Output Determination 97

Chapter 11
The Pursuit of Self-Interest —
Rational Expectations, New Classical Macroeconomics, and Efficient Markets 108

Chapter 12
Rational Wage Stickiness —
Modern Keynesian Theory with Rational Expectations 120

Chapter 13
Market Failures versus Perfect Markets —
New Keynesians versus Real-Business-Cycle Theorists 134

Chapter 14
What Should Policymakers Do? —
Objectives and Targets of Macroeconomic Policy 147

Chapter 15
What Can Policymakers Accomplish? —
Rules versus Discretion in Macroeconomic Policy 159

Chapter 16
Policymaking in the World Economy —
International Dimensions of Macroeconomic Policy 171

Answers to Questions 183

Preface

This study guide is designed as a learning aid for students using the third edition of *Macroeconomics: Theories, Policies, and International Applications*, by Roger LeRoy Miller and David D. VanHoose.

The goal of the study guide is to assist students in developing a clearer understanding of macroeconomic theory and its application to domestic and international issues. To help students in this endeavor, the study guide summarizes the contents of each chapter and lists key terms and concepts, which students can define in their own words. Students can test their understanding of the contents of each chapter by answering self-test questions (20 multiple-choice questions and 10 short-answer questions per chapter). The answers to all questions appear at the end of the study guide.

I welcome comments and suggestions from all users of this study guide.

David VanHoose

Chapter 1: The Macroeconomy

Chapter Summary

Macroeconomics is the study of the entire economy. There are two distinguishing features of macroeconomics. One of these is the focus that macroeconomics places on aggregate variables. The other is its natural concern with the issue of money's role in the economy, given that people use money to make nearly all transactions.

There are two key sets of macroeconomic variables. Domestic variables include measures of overall economic activity within a nation, including the nation's total output, employment, and unemployment and its money growth and inflation rates. International variables provide indications of a nation's economic interactions with the rest of the world. These include a nation's trade balance and the rates at which its currency may be exchanged for currencies of other nations.

There are five key issues in macroeconomics. One is isolating the factors that determine a nation's long-term growth in output and employment, which, as shown in Figure 1, tend to move together. A comparison of the world's nations and regions indicates considerable variation in economic growth. Macroeconomists seek to understand why these variations occur.

Figure 1: U.S. Output and Employment

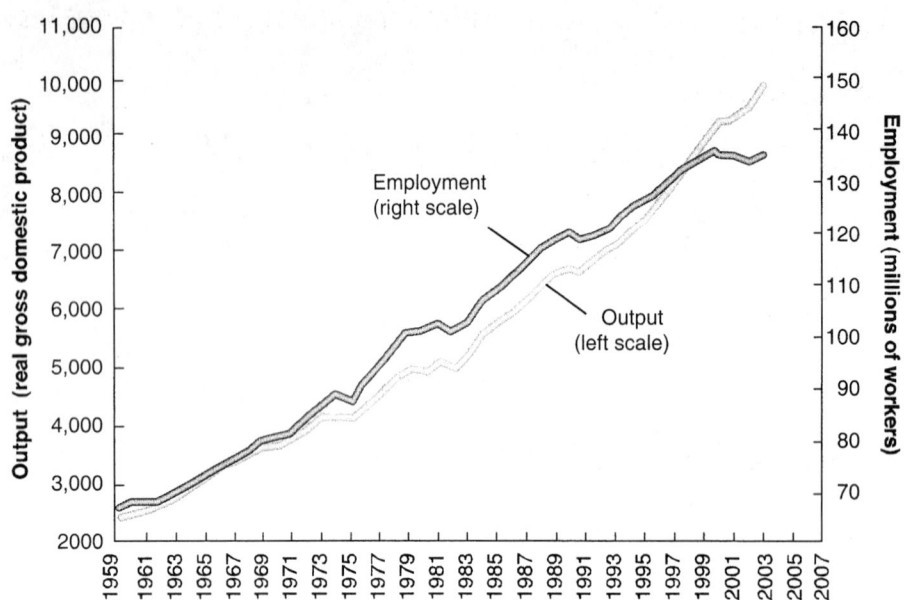

A second important issue is explaining short-run variations in output and employment. Such cyclical volatility in economic activity is associated with changes in aggregate unemployment and with short-term variations in a nation's average standard of living.

A third issue is determining the extent to which changes in the quantity of money influence a nation's output, employment, and prices. Historical experience indicates that, at times, variations in the amount of money in circulation have been associated with changes in these aggregate variables.

A fourth fundamental issue concerns policymaking. Understanding the interrelationships among macroeconomic variables is necessary if we are to identify appropriate objectives of macroeconomic policymaking and to determine the best approaches to implementing macroeconomic policies.

The final key issue in macroeconomics is resolving how international elements, such as exchange rates and cross-border trade in goods and services affect a nation's economic performance. This is a particularly important issue as nations increasingly become more interdependent.

Two features of macroeconomics make it a controversial subject. First, macroeconomists often disagree about how much aggregation is appropriate for analyzing the determinants of overall economic activity. Second, macroeconomists cannot test their theories using controlled experiments. Consequently, they must examine aggregate observations of artificially constructed measures of economic activity. These features of macroeconomics naturally produce different interpretations and foster controversies.

Key Terms and Concepts

Aggregation
Domestic variables
Exchange rate
General equilibrium analysis
International trade
Macroeconomic variables
Macroeconomics
Merchandise balance of trade
Merchandise exports
Merchandise imports
Microeconomic foundations
Microeconomics
Standard of living
Unemployment

Multiple-Choice Questions

1. Macroeconomics is the branch of economics that considers

    I. a nation's total economic activity.
    II. aggregate domestic and international variables.
    III. resource allocation in individual markets for goods.

    A) I only
    B) III only
    C) both I and II
    D) both II and III

2. Which of the following statements best summarizes the current relationship between microeconomics and macroeconomics?

    A) The two general areas of economic studies are completely unrelated.
    B) The two general areas of economic studies essentially examine identical issues.
    C) Most macroeconomists regard microeconomics as a key foundation for their theories.
    D) Most macroeconomists follow microeconomists by trying to understand each individual component of the aggregate economy.

3. Aggregation, which is a key feature of macroeconomics, refers to

    A) the act of adding together individual economic components to obtain totals for the economy as a whole.
    B) the tendency for modern macroeconomic theories to be based on microeconomic foundations.
    C) a process by which key macroeconomic variables such as output and employment are expressed in dollar terms to provide a common basis of comparison.
    D) the tendency for the economies of the world's nations to become more interdependent, thereby increasing the scope for interrelationships among key macroeconomic variables.

4. Which of the following is particularly important in the development of macroeconomic theories?

    A) explaining the allocation of total income between profits and wages
    B) explaining the role of variations in the amount of money in circulation
    C) taking into account the existence of government assistance programs
    D) taking into account the magnitude of national health-care expenditures

5. Distinguishing features of macroeconomics are its

   A) emphasis on the distribution and allocation of scarce resources.
   B) consideration of individual markets for goods, services, and money.
   C) focus on the utility maximizing by individual consumers and profit maximizing by individual producers.
   D) consideration of aggregate measures of economic performance and the role of the amount of money in circulation.

6. Macroeconomic variables are

   A) summary measures of overall economic activity.
   B) summary measures of production in individual markets.
   C) index measures of the average amounts that consumers spend on a particular good.
   D) index measures of allocations of income and wealth among different classes of consumers.

7. Between 1959 and 2003, total employment in the United States roughly

   A) stayed the same.
   B) increased by a multiple factor of two.
   C) increased by a multiple factor of three.
   D) increased by a multiple factor of four.

8. The overall capability of an average resident of a nation to consume goods and services is a key indicator of the nation's

   A) price level.
   B) inflation rate.
   C) exchange rate.
   D) standard of living.

9. If a nation's labor productivity increases from one year to the next, then we may conclude that, if the nation's population remains unchanged,

   A) its residents will have to work more hours to produce the same amount of output.
   B) its residents will be able to produce and consume more goods and services.
   C) there must be a decline in aggregate business profits.
   D) there must be a decline in workers' wage earnings.

10. Which of the following is true about U.S. unemployment?

    I. It can exhibit considerable year-to-year variation.
    II. This term refers to underutilized machines and factories.
    III. This term applies only to workers in manufacturing industries.

    A) I only
    B) II only
    C) both I and III
    D) both II and III

11. Which of the following is true about U.S. money growth rates and inflation rates?

    A) Higher inflation always accompanies increases in money growth rates.
    B) Lower inflation always accompanies increases in money growth rates.
    C) During some periods the two variables appear to be related, but during other periods they do not.
    D) Inflation rates measure annual changes in the price level, while money growth rates measure annual changes in inflation rates.

12. The merchandise balance of trade is

    A) purchases of foreign goods and services minus sales of home goods and services abroad.
    B) sales of home goods and services abroad minus purchases of foreign goods and services.
    C) purchases of foreign goods minus sales of home goods abroad.
    D) sales of home goods abroad minus purchases of foreign goods.

13. A merchandise trade deficit occurs whenever

    A) exports of physical goods exceed imports of physical goods.
    B) imports of physical goods exceed exports of physical goods.
    C) sales of goods and services abroad exceed purchases of foreign goods and services.
    D) purchases of foreign goods and services exceed sales of goods and services abroad.

14. Of the following nations, which recently has experienced per capita output levels closest to the world's average per capita output?

    A) China
    B) Nigeria
    C) the United States
    D) the Czech Republic

15. Of the following nations or regions, which has been the slowest-growing in recent years?

    A) Japan
    B) United States
    C) Western Hemisphere
    D) Eastern Europe /Middle East

16. Of the following regions, which has experienced the highest average inflation rates in recent years?

    A) developing nations in Asia
    B) United States
    C) Africa
    D) Japan

17. Which of the following statements is correct?

    I. As compared with other nations, the United States has the largest share of the world's output.
    II. The U.S. share of world output has leveled off in recent years.
    III. World output has declined steadily since World War II.

    A) I only
    B) III only
    C) both I and II
    D) both II and III

18. In comparing the United States and the European Union, which of the following statements is incorrect?

    A) European Union unemployment rates have tended to lie below U.S. unemployment rates.
    B) Both regions have experienced similar unemployment rates.
    C) Total employment fell in the United States during the 1990s.
    D) Employment stagnated in the European Union in the 1990s.

19. As compared with other areas of study in economics, which of the following features makes macroeconomics relatively controversial?

    I. Its consideration of policy issues.
    II. Its consideration of aggregate variables.
    III. The inability of macroeconomists to conduct controlled experiments.

    A) I and II only
    B) II and III only
    C) I and III only
    D) I, II, and III

20. Which of the following is true of macroeconomic data?

    A) They are subject to few controversies.
    B) They are artificially constructed aggregates.
    C) They are subject to no measurement errors.
    D) They can be generated in a laboratory setting.

Short-Answer Questions

1. Which branch of economics would study the allocations of resources by a firm?

2. Which branch of economics would study the determination of total employment?

3. What is the term describing the effort to base macroeconomics on the principles of microeconomics?

4. What is the act of summing up all individual components of an economy to obtain a measure of total economic activity?

5. In general, what is the name of summary measures of total economic activity only *within* a nation's borders?

6. What is the broad term for exchanges of goods across national boundaries?

7. What do economists call the overall capability of a typical resident of a nation to produce and consume goods and services?

8. What occurs if a nation's merchandise trade balance is positive?

9. In recent years, has China's per capita output been above, below, or right at the world average?

10. In recent years, has Germany's per capita output been above, below, or right at the world average?

Chapter 2: How Do We Know How We're Doing? — Measuring Macroeconomic Variables

Chapter Summary

Economists use gross domestic product (GDP) to measure a nation's total output of goods and services. GDP the value, at market prices, of all *final* goods and services produced within the nation's borders during a specific period. GDP excludes nonmarket transactions and exchanges of financial assets, and it does not account for possible adverse effects of economic growth.

The national income accounts, which are the formal tabulations of the nation's income and product, use two approaches to computing GDP. One of these is the product approach, which entails adding together four types of spending on final goods and services produced during a given year: (1) consumption spending by households, (2) gross investment spending, including business spending on new capital goods, net accumulations of inventories of newly produced goods, and expenditures on residential construction, (3) total expenditures on goods and services by state, local, and federal governments, and (4) net export spending, or total spending on domestically produced goods and services by residents of other nations minus expenditures on foreign-produced goods and services by home residents that do not constitute spending on home production.

In contrast, the income approach to calculating GDP adds up all sources of income resulting from current production of goods and services. This approach proceeds in four steps. Economists begin by adding together wages and salaries, interest income, rental income, and profits of businesses to obtain the total factor earnings in the economy, called national income. Then, economists add indirect taxes and transfer payments to businesses to national income to obtain the economy's net national product. Next, they add depreciation to obtain gross national product (GNP). Finally, they add net income earned by foreign residents from U.S.-based production to net national product. This gives the amount of GDP.

To trace flows of payments across nations' borders, economists use a system of accounting known as the balance of payments accounts. In these accounts, any international transaction entailing a payment by a U.S. resident, company, or government agency appears as a negative entry. Any transaction leading to a receipt by a U.S. resident, company, or government agency appears as a positive entry.

There are three separate accounts in the balance of payments. One of these, the current account, tabulates international trade and transfers of goods and services and flows of income. One component of the U.S. current account is the merchandise balance of trade, which tabulates sales of physical goods by U.S. firms to residents of other nations (merchandise export) minus the value of physical goods that U.S. residents purchase from foreign firms (merchandise imports). The current account balance is the sum of the merchandise trade balance, net international exchanges of services, international flows of income receipts to U.S. residents net of payments abroad by U.S. residents, and net unilateral transfers to U.S. residents.

The second balance of payments account, called the private capital account, tabulates changes in private asset holdings by U.S. residents abroad and by foreigners in the United States. Acquisitions of foreign assets by U.S. residents, such purchases of shares of ownership of plants or equipment located abroad or purchases of foreign securities such as bonds are positive entries in the U.S. capital account. Foreign acquisitions of such assets within U.S. borders are negative entries. The net total of all asset changes for individuals and businesses is the capital account balance.

The sum of the current account balance and the private capital account balance is the private payments balance, which gives the net total of all private exchanges between U.S. individuals and businesses and the rest of the world. A negative value for the private payments balance indicates a private payments deficit, which is sometimes called a "balance of payments deficit." A positive value for the private payments balance indicates a private payments surplus, which is sometimes called a "balance of payments surplus."

Asset transactions of governmental agencies appear in the official settlements balance, which is the third account within the balance of payments. Purchases of foreign assets or overseas deposits of funds by the U.S. Treasury, the Federal Reserve, or any agencies of the U.S. government are receipts that appear as positive entries in the U.S. official settlements balance. Acquisitions of U.S. assets or deposits by foreign central banks or governments are outflows and appear as negative entries in this account. The total net amount of all governmental and central bank transactions is the official settlements balance. In the absence of a statistical discrepancy, the private payments balance and the official settlements balances must sum zero. That is, the overall balance of payments must equal zero, because any exchange of goods, services, income, or assets abroad yields corresponding positive and negative entries in the balance of payments accounts.

To address the problem with making year-to-year comparisons of inflation-distorted GDP figures, economists use real gross domestic product (real GDP), which accounts for price changes and thereby reflects more accurately the value of an economy's output net of artificial increases resulting from inflation. The unadjusted measure of GDP is nominal gross domestic product (nominal GDP), which is calculated in current dollar terms with no adjustment for effects of price changes. If y denotes real GDP and P denotes a measure of the overall price level, then nominal GDP, denoted Y, thereby must equal $Y = y \times P$. That is, nominal GDP equals real GDP times a measure of the overall price level. The factor P is the GDP price deflator. The reference year for the GDP price deflator is the base year, which is a year in which nominal GDP is equal to real GDP ($Y = y$), so that the GDP deflator's value is one ($P = 1$). As shown in panel (a) of Figure 2, because real GDP is adjusted for price changes, it has grown less noticeably than nominal GDP as the price level has risen since the 1950s.

Figure 2: U.S. Nominal GDP, Real GDP, and Price Indexes

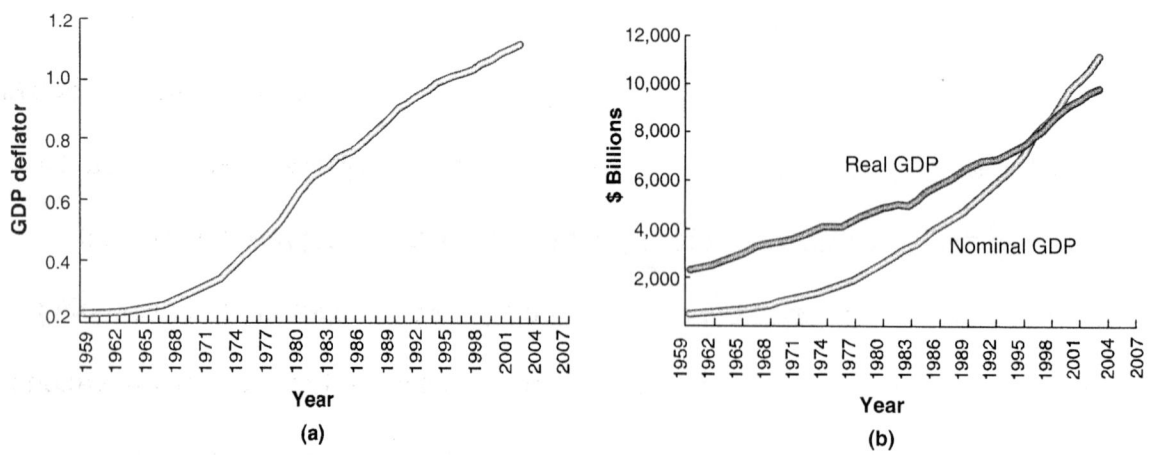

Using a fixed-base-year measure of real GDP ignores the fact that as prices change, households and businesses reallocate their purchases by buying fewer of the goods and services whose prices rise the most and more of the goods and services whose prices rise the least. Consequently, output increases most for those goods and services whose prices increase by the least amount. To counteract the slight bias in measured growth in real output that results, at the end of 1995 the U.S. government began tabulating chain-weight real GDP, meaning that the government computes real GDP using prices in both for the year in question and the preceding year as weights.

Alternatives to the GDP price deflator as a measure of the overall price level are fixed-weight price indexes that economists tabulate as a weighted average of the prices of these of a fixed group, or "basket," of goods and services. A key fixed-weight price index is the consumer price index (CPI), which is a weighted sum of prices of about 95,000 items that the government determines a typical U.S. consumer purchases each year. Panel (b) of Figure 2 shows that the CPI and the GDP deflator tend to move together. Another fixed-weight price index is the producer price index (PPI), which is a weighted average of prices of goods that a typical business firm purchases from other businesses and then uses in its own production process.

The U.S. government uses the CPI to adjust government benefits, such as Social Security payments, to account for price changes. One problem with relying on a fixed-weight price index such as the CPI for such benefit adjustments, however, is that relative prices of goods change over time, inducing people to change their spending allocations by substituting among goods. Another problem is that product innovations that lead to the development and sale of new goods and services are not readily included in the CPI market basket. The use of fixed weights also ignores quality changes that may take place over time. Finally, the government uses list prices, or the prices that businesses formally print in catalogs and price lists, even though many purchases actually take place at discount prices. A 1995 Congressional commission concluded that CPI annual inflation rates have been nearly 1 percentage point higher as a result of these problems.

Key Terms and Concepts

Base year
Balance of payments accounts
Capital account
Capital good
Chain-weight real GDP
Circular flow diagram
Consumer price index (CPI)
Consumption spending
Current account
Depreciation
Fixed-weight price index
Flexible-weight price index
GDP price deflator
Government spending
Gross domestic product (GDP)
Investment spending
National income
National income accounts
Net domestic product (NDP)
Net export spending
Nominal gross domestic product (nominal GDP)
Official settlements balance
Private payments balance
Producer price index (PPI)
Real gross domestic product (real GDP)

Multiple-Choice Questions

1. Gross domestic product is the

   A) market value of all goods and services produced within the nation's borders during a given period.
   B) value of all cross-border exchanges undertaken by a nation's residents during a given period.
   C) value of all transactions that take place within a nation's borders during a specific interval.
   D) value of all manufactured output produced within a nation's borders during a given period.

2. For a given year, which of the following is included in gross domestic product?

   I. foreign residents' earnings from home production during that year
   II. home residents' earnings from production abroad during that year
   III. the value of intermediate goods used in final goods produced during that year

   A) I only
   B) III only
   C) both I and II
   D) both II and III

3. Which one of the following statements about gross domestic product (GDP) is correct?

   A) GDP excludes foreign residents' earnings from home production.
   B) GDP includes the value of intermediate goods not yet used in final goods.
   C) GDP includes all capital-account transactions in the balance of payments.
   D) GDP excludes all current-account transactions in the balance of payments.

4. In the national income accounts, which of the following must be subtracted from gross domestic product to obtain national income?

   I. depreciation
   II. indirect taxes
   III. income earned by foreign residents from home production net of income that home residents earn from foreign production

   A) both I and II only
   B) both II and III only
   C) both I and III only
   D) I, II, and III

5. Which of the following is excluded from gross domestic product?

    A) the value of inventory investment by business firms
    B) net merchandise exports in the balance of payments
    C) foreign residents' earnings of income from home production
    D) the value of services performed by unpaid housewives or househusbands

6. Which of the following is true of gross domestic product (GDP)?

    A) GDP is a measure of the overall welfare of a nation's citizens.
    B) A rise in GDP indicates an improvement in a nation's quality of life.
    C) GDP is a measure of a nation's total output of goods and services.
    D) An increase in GDP must be unrelated to international transactions.

7. If the a U.S. business firm were to sell pharmaceuticals to a government in another country that pays for the reactor with a check drawn on an account with the U.S. Federal Reserve System, then which of the following items would be recorded in the U.S. balance of payments?

    A) a negative entry in the current account; a positive entry in the private capital account
    B) a negative entry in the current account; a positive entry in the official settlements balance
    C) a positive entry in the current account; a negative entry in the private capital account
    D) a positive entry in the current account; a negative entry in the official settlements balance

8. If a U.S. resident were to sell a share of stock issued by a U.S. firm three years ago to a foreign resident today, and if the foreign resident were to pay for the share by writing a check drawn on an account with a U.S. bank branch located in her country, then which of the following items would be recorded in the U.S. balance of payments?

    A) a negative entry to the current account; a positive entry to the private capital account
    B) a positive entry to the current account; a negative entry tot he private capital account
    C) offsetting positive entries and negative entries in the private capital account
    D) offsetting positive entries and negative entries in the current account

9. Which of the following is included in the merchandise trade balance?

   I.   exports and imports of goods
   II. flows of services across national borders
   III. flows of incomes across national borders

   A) I only
   B) III only
   C) both I and III
   D) both II and III

10. Which of the following is excluded from the current account?

    I.   flows of services across national borders
    II. flows of incomes across national borders
    III. business investment in new factories in other nations

    A) I only
    B) III only
    C) both I and III
    D) both II and III

11. In the absence of a statistical discrepancy, when does a private payments deficit occur?

    A) when the official settlements balance is negative
    B) when the official settlements balance is positive
    C) when the sum of the private capital account balance and the current account balance is positive
    D) when the sum of the private capital account balance and the current account balance is equal to zero

12. In the absence of a statistical discrepancy, a nation always experiences a current account deficit whenever

    I.   the sum of net exports, net flows of services abroad, net income flows into the nation, and net unilateral transfers to the nation is less than zero
    II. the private capital account balance and official settlements balance both are greater than zero
    III. the overall balance of payments is equal to zero

    A) I only
    B) III only
    C) both I and II
    D) both II and III

13. In the absence of a statistical discrepancy, if a nation's official settlements balance is equal to zero, then

    I.   its private payments balance is equal to zero
    II. its overall balance of payments is greater than zero
    III. the sum of its current account balance and its capital account balance is equal to zero.

    A) I only
    B) II only
    C) both I and III
    D) both II and III

14. Real GDP is equal to

    A) nominal GDP times the GDP price deflator.
    B) nominal GDP times the consumer price index.
    C) nominal GDP divided by the GDP price deflator.
    D) nominal GDP divided by base-year nominal GDP.

15. If a nation's real GDP were to decline and its nominal GDP were to rise during a three-year period, then it must be true that during this period,

    A) the nation experienced inflation.
    B) the value of the nation's GDP deflator declined.
    C) the value of the nation's consumer price index fell.
    D) the base year for computing GDP must have been the middle year.

16. Of the following statements about the consumer price index (CPI), which is correct?

    A) The basket of goods used to compute the CPI automatically adjusts each year.
    B) By definition, the CPI is equal to nominal GDP divided by real GDP.
    C) By definition, the CPI is equal to real GDP divided by nominal GDP.
    D) The CPI is a fixed-weight price index.

17. The GDP price deflator is

    A) equal to real GDP divided by nominal GDP.
    B) equal to real GDP times nominal GDP.
    C) a flexible-weight price index.
    D) a fixed-weight price index.

18. Which of the following is widely recognized to be a difficulty in inferring inflation using the consumer price index?

    I. Quality changes distort the interpretation of prices of the CPI basket of goods.
    II. The CPI is constructed with list prices, even though consumers often pay discount prices.
    III. Development of new goods changes the basket of goods that people actually consume, but the CPI goods basket is changed infrequently.

    A) both I and II
    B) both I and III
    C) both II and III
    D) I, II, and III

19. Chain-weight GDP reduces distortions in output-growth tabulations by

    A) ignoring the effects of price changes.
    B) using current and prior-year prices as weights in computing real GDP.
    C) varying the base year of real GDP computations on even-numbered years.
    D) using the consumer price index as the fixed-weight index for all real GDP calculations.

20. Suppose that 1996 is the base year and that 1996 nominal GDP was equal to $7.8 trillion. In addition, suppose that nominal GDP in 1995 was equal to $7.4 trillion. Which of the following statements is correct?

    A) The 1996 GDP price deflator was equal to 1, and real GDP in 1996 was equal to $7.8 trillion /1 = $7.8 trillion.
    B) The 1996 GDP price deflator was equal to 0.4, and real GDP in 1996 was equal to $7.8 trillion /0.4 = $19.5 trillion.
    C) The 1995 GDP price deflator was equal to 0.4, and real GDP in 1995 was equal to $7.4 trillion × 0.4 = $2.96 trillion.
    D) The 1995 GDP price deflator was equal to 1, and real GDP in 1995 was equal to $7.8 trillion / $7.4 trillion = $1.054 trillion.

Short-Answer Questions

1. What is the term for the value of productive equipment that is used up or worn out as part of the production process and that must be replaced to maintain the same amount of equipment?

2. What is a capital good?

3. What account in the balance of payments tabulates international trade and transfers of goods and services and flows of income?

4. Where in the balance of payments do economists tabulate asset transactions involving governmental agencies?

5. In a nation's balance of payments, what is the private payments balance?

6. What is the value of any nation's overall balance of payments?

7. What is the formula for calculating the value of the GDP price deflator?

8. What is a real-world example of a fixed-weight price index?

9. What current measure of real output seeks to avoid distortions in growth calculations by using prices from current and prior years as weights?

10. If nominal GDP were to decline while real GDP increased, what direction would the price level move during the period in question?

Chapter 3: The Self-Adjusting Economy — Classical Macroeconomic Theory: Employment, Output, and Prices

Chapter Summary

The classical model, which stems from the 18th century, was the first systematic and rigorous attempt to explain the determinants of macroeconomic variables such as aggregate employment, real GDP, and the price level. Three key assumptions provide a foundation for the classical macroeconomic theory. One of these is that people rationally pursue their own self-interest. Another is that people do not experience money illusion, meaning they are not fooled by current-dollar changes that leave their real incomes unaffected. Finally, markets for goods, services, and factors of production are purely competitive, so that there are large numbers of buyers and sellers, which individually cannot influence market prices.

According to the classical model, the amount of labor employed in the economy is determined by labor-market equilibrium. The demand for labor stems directly from the marginal product of labor, or the additional output produced by an additional unit of labor, which in turn derives from the aggregate production function relating the quantities of factors of production to total production of real output by all firms in the economy. Real and money wages adjust to maintain equality between the quantity of labor supplied by workers and the quantity of labor demanded by firms. Then the equilibrium amount of real aggregate output is the amount that firms can produce with this quantity of labor, given the firms' use of other factors of production and available technology. The equilibrium money wage adjusts in equal proportion to changes in prices, so employment and output do not change when the price varies. This means that the classical aggregate supply schedule is vertical.

The classical theory of price-level determination depends on the quantity theory of money, the good that functions as medium of exchange, store of value, unit of account, and standard of deferred payment. The basis of the quantity theory of money is the equation of exchange, $M \times V \equiv P \times y$, where V denotes the income velocity of money, or the average number of times people spend each unit of money on final goods and services per unit of time, and where both sides of the equation measure the current-dollar value of monetary payments for final goods and services. If velocity is sufficiently stable that it may be regarded as a constant, then this implies the Cambridge-equation theory of the demand for money, $M^d = k \times Y = k \times P \times y$, where k is the reciprocal of the constant velocity. If people hold the quantity of money placed into circulation by the central bank, then the result is a downward-sloping set of combinations of the price level and real output called the aggregate demand schedule. The equation for this schedule is $y^d = M / (k \times P)$.

The equilibrium price level is the price level that maintains equality of the quantity of real output demanded and the amount of real output supplied by firms. This price level arises at the point at which the aggregate demand schedule, whose position is determined by the quantity of money in circulation and the income velocity of money, crosses the vertical classical aggregate supply schedule. An increase in the price level, or inflation, can arise from two fundamental sources in the classical model. One, illustrated in panel (a) of Figure 3, is a decline in aggregate supply, caused perhaps by a reduction in labor force participation, a fall in labor productivity, higher marginal tax rates on wages, or the provision of government benefits that give households incentives not to supply labor services to firms. The other possible source of inflation, illustrated in panel (b), is an increase in aggregate demand, perhaps because of a decline in the income velocity of money or by an increase in the quantity of money in circulation. Because the aggregate supply schedule actually shifts rightward in a growing economy, and because the velocity of money has not declined considerably, the classical theory indicates that the main explanation for a positive trend inflation rate in recent decades has been excessive money growth.

Figure 3: Sources of Inflation in the Classical Model

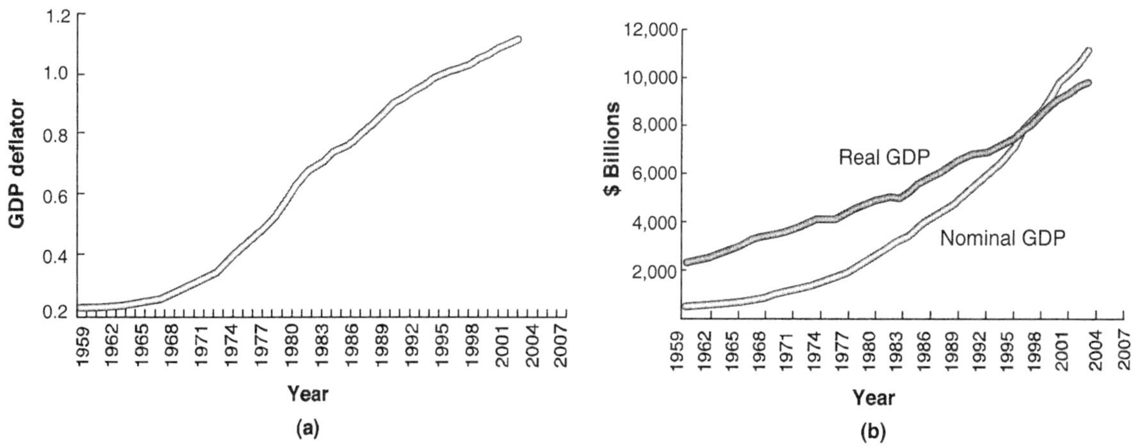

(a)

(b)

Key Terms and Concepts

Aggregate demand schedule (y^d)
Aggregate supply schedule (y^s)
Barter
Cambridge equation
Equation of exchange
Income velocity of money
Law of diminishing marginal returns
Marginal product of labor
Medium of exchange

Money
Money illusion
Production function
Pure competition
Quantity theory of money
Standard of deferred payment
Store of value
Unit of account
Value of the marginal product of labor

Multiple-Choice Questions

1. Which one of the following is not a key assumption of the classical model?

   A) pure competition
   B) rational self-interest
   C) stable quantity of money
   D) absence of money illusion

2. Along an economy's aggregate production function, which of the following is not fixed in the short run?

   A) land
   B) labor
   C) capital
   D) entrepreneurship

3. Which one of the following statements best explains why the aggregate production function is bowed downward, or concave?

   A) Each additional one-unit increase in the amount of labor employed yields a smaller increase in the production of real output.
   B) Each additional one-unit increase in the amount of labor employed yields a larger increase in the production of real output.
   C) Any increase in real output requires an increase in employment.
   D) Any increase in real output requires a reduction in employment.

4. Which one of the following statements best explains why the marginal-product-of-labor (MP_N) schedule slopes downward?

   A) Each additional one-unit increase in the amount of labor employed yields a smaller increase in the production of real output.
   B) Each additional one-unit increase in the amount of labor employed yields a larger increase in the production of real output.
   C) Any increase in real output requires an increase in employment.
   D) Any increase in real output requires a reduction in employment.

5. By definition, the value of labor's marginal product is equal to

   A) the additional profit that a firm earns by hiring an additional unit of labor.
   B) the additional cost that a firm incurs by hiring an additional unit of labor.
   C) the marginal cost times the marginal product of labor.
   D) the output price times the marginal product of labor.

6. The underlying reason that the marginal product schedule is a purely competitive firm's labor demand schedule is that

   A) a purely competitive firm produces output up to the point at which price equals marginal revenue, which by definition is equal to marginal cost in the classical macroeconomic model.
   B) a purely competitive firm produces output up to the point at which price equals marginal cost, which in turn is equal to the wage rate divided by the marginal product of labor.
   C) workers increase the amount of labor services that they supply to firms as the real wage rises.
   D) workers increase the amount of labor services that they supply to firms as the real wage falls.

7. In the classical model, real output is supply determined because

   A) a decline in the price level induces a rise in the equilibrium real wage that causes equilibrium output to fall.
   B) a decline in the price level induces a reduction in the equilibrium real wage that causes equilibrium output to increase.
   C) a rise in the price level causes the equilibrium real wage to increase by a more-than-proportionate amount, so that output stays fixed.
   D) a rise in the price level causes the equilibrium nominal wage to rise in equal proportion, leaving equilibrium employment unchanged.

8. Which of the following statements about the classical aggregate supply schedule is correct?

   I. The classical aggregate supply schedule is vertical.
   II. Along the classical aggregate supply schedule, the state of technology in the economy varies as the price level changes.
   III. Along the classical aggregate supply schedule, the quantity of real output produced is consistent with an equalized quantity of labor supplied by workers and quantity of labor demanded by firms.

   A) II only
   B) III only
   C) both I and II
   D) both I and III

9. If more workers enter the labor force, bringing about an increase in the supply of labor at any given real wage rate, then there is a

   A) movement upward along the classical aggregate supply schedule.
   B) movement downward along the classical aggregate supply schedule.
   C) leftward shift in the position of the classical aggregate supply schedule.
   D) rightward shift in the position of the classical aggregate supply schedule.

10. Which of the following statements about the classical aggregate demand schedule is correct?

   I. The classical aggregate demand schedule is vertical.
   II. Along the classical aggregate demand schedule, the quantity of money and the income velocity of money have constant values.
   III. Along the classical aggregate demand schedule, the quantity of labor demanded by firms equals the quantity of labor supplied by workers.

   A) II only
   B) III only
   C) both I and II
   D) both I and III

11. A sudden increase in the price level results in a

   A) movement upward along the classical aggregate demand schedule.
   B) movement downward along the classical aggregate demand schedule.
   C) leftward shift in the position of the classical aggregate demand schedule.
   D) rightward shift in the position of the classical aggregate demand schedule.

12. A reduction in the income velocity of money results in a

   A) movement upward along the classical aggregate demand schedule.
   B) movement downward along the classical aggregate demand schedule.
   C) leftward shift in the position of the classical aggregate demand schedule.
   D) rightward shift in the position of the classical aggregate demand schedule.

13. Which of the following is a function of money?

   I. store of value
   II. medium of exchange
   III. standard of deferred payment

   A) both I and II only
   B) both I and III only
   C) both II and III only
   D) I, II, and III

14. In 1945-46 Hungary, residents used a currency called the "pengo" to purchase goods and services, which were priced in units of this currency. Inflation became such a problem, however, that the government created special "tax pengo" deposit accounts that were indexed to inflation. Most Hungarian residents held funds in these accounts instead of in accounts denominated in regular pengos, and they denominated most debts in terms of tax pengos instead of regular pengos. It may be concluded that the regular pengo currency functioned as a _____ and as a _____.

    A) store of value; medium of exchange
    B) unit of account; medium of exchange
    C) store of value; standard of deferred payment
    D) unit of account; standard of deferred payment

15. In the situation describe in question 14, the tax pengo functioned as a _____ and as a _____.

    A) store of value; medium of exchange
    B) unit of account; medium of exchange
    C) store of value; standard of deferred payment
    D) unit of account; standard of deferred payment

16. Along the classical aggregate demand schedule,

    A) people in the economy are willing to supply exactly the quantity of labor demanded by firms.
    B) people in the economy are willing to hold the quantity of money placed in circulation.
    C) the income velocity of money decreases as the price level rises.
    D) the income velocity of money increases as the price level rises.

17. In the classical model, one possible explanation for inflation would be

    A) a steady increase in real output through continuing increases in aggregate supply via technological improvement.
    B) a steady increase in real output through rightward shifts in aggregate supply owing to immigration of new workers.
    C) a rise in aggregate demand induced by a fall in the income velocity of money.
    D) an increase in aggregate demand induced by a reduction in the money stock.

18. According to the classical model, a technological improvement would, if all other factors were unchanged, cause

    I.   a decline in the equilibrium price level.
    II. a rise in the equilibrium level of real output.
    III. a rightward shift of the aggregate demand schedule.

    A) I only
    B) III only
    C) both I and II
    D) both II and III

19. According to the classical model, emigration that induced a decline in a nation's labor force would, if all other factors were unchanged, cause

    I.   a rise in the equilibrium price level.
    II. a rightward shift in the labor demand schedule.
    III. a rightward shift in the aggregate supply schedule.

    A) I only
    B) III only
    C) both I and II
    D) both II and III

20. According to the classical model, a rise in the equilibrium price level

    A) could result from an increase in the quantity of money that brought about a downward movement along the aggregate demand schedule.
    B) could result from immigration that increased the quantity of labor supplied at any given real wage rate.
    C) would bring about a rightward shift in the aggregate supply schedule's position.
    D) would bring about an upward movement along the aggregate supply schedule.

Short-Answer Questions

1. What is the term for a situation in which an individual supplies more labor because she observes a rise in the nominal wage, even though an equiproportionate price-level increase also takes place?

2. What is the marginal product of labor?

3. What is the law of diminishing marginal returns?

4. In the classical model, what schedule shows all combinations of real output and the price level that maintain labor-market equilibrium?

5. What schedule displaying price level-real output combinations stems from the Cambridge equation for the demand for money?

6. What is the name of the equation, $M \times V \equiv P \times y$?

7. What function does money perform when people set it aside as wealth that they anticipate will maintain its value over time?

8. What function does money perform when prices of goods and services are quoted in terms of money?

9. What function does money perform when debts are quoted in terms of money?

10. According to what relationship are people's holdings of money equal to a constant fraction of their income?

Chapter 4: Classical Macroeconomic Theory — Interest Rates and Exchange Rates

Chapter Summary

The real interest rate is equal to the nominal interest rate minus the expected rate of inflation. In the classical model, the real interest rate adjusts to equalize the quantity of loanable funds supplied, or aggregate private saving, with the quantity of loanable funds demanded, or the sum of total desired private investment and the government deficit. An increase in the government's budget deficit, which equals any amount of government spending in excess of tax revenues, raises the demand for loanable funds. This causes a crowding-out effect as the resulting rise in the real interest rate induces a decrease in private spending.

A rise in a government budget surplus, which equals any amount of tax revenues in excess of government spending, increases the supply of loanable funds. This pushes down the equilibrium real interest rate and generates an increase in private spending.

The nominal interest rate equals the real interest rate, which in the classical model is determined in the market for loanable funds, plus the expected rate of inflation. A rise in the anticipated rate of growth of the quantity of money in circulation causes expected inflation to rise. This, in turn, brings about a rise in the nominal interest rate.

The exchange rate is the value of one nation's currency in terms of the currency of another nation. The classical theory's foundation for understanding how exchange rates are determined is purchasing power parity. According to the purchasing power parity doctrine, international arbitrage equalizes the price level in one nation with the foreign price level times the exchange rate. Consequently, as shown in Figure 4, output-market equilibrium in a home nation determines the home nation's price level and output-market equilibrium in a foreign country determines the foreign price level. Then the exchange rate adjusts to maintain purchasing power parity. Persistent inflation in the home nation caused by an excessive rate of growth of the amount of home money in circulation thereby will be accompanied by persistent depreciation in, or decline in the value of, the home nation's currency.

Figure 4: Exchange Rate Determination in the Classical Model

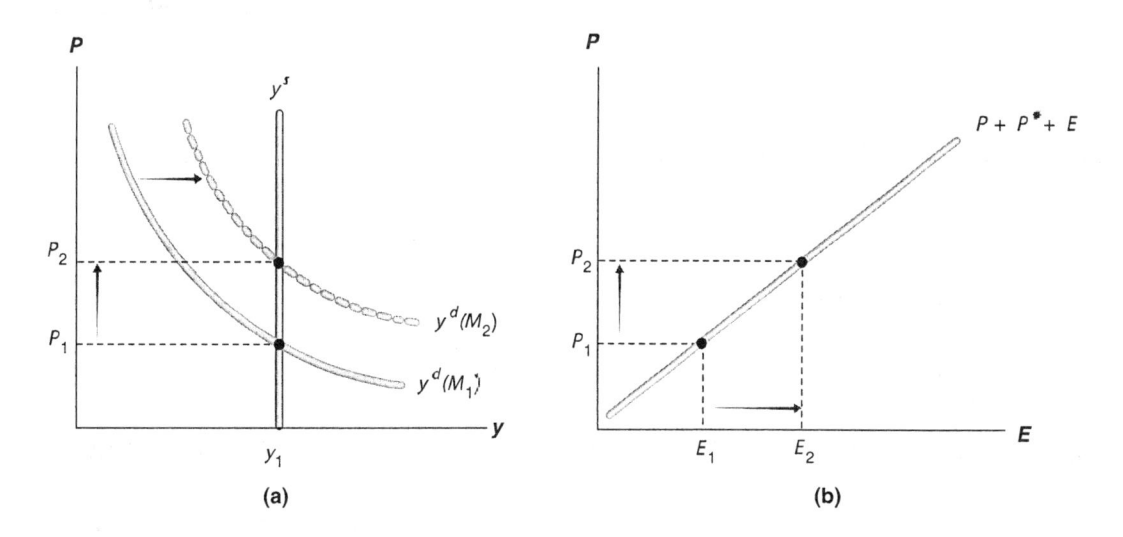

Key Terms and Concepts

Appreciation
Closed economy
Crowding-out effect
Depreciation
Fiscal policy
International arbitrage
Open economy
Purchasing power parity
Real interest rate

Multiple-Choice Questions

1. The real interest rate is equal to

   A) the nominal interest rate minus the expected inflation rate.
   B) the nominal interest rate plus the expected inflation rate.
   C) the nominal interest rate minus the actual inflation rate.
   D) the nominal interest rate plus the actual inflation rate.

2. In the classical model, an increase in the real interest rate generates

   A) a decrease in a government budget deficit.
   B) an increase in a government budget surplus.
   C) a rightward shift in the demand for loanable funds.
   D) an upward movement along the loanable funds supply schedule.

3. In the classical model, if desired investment spending increases at any given interest rate, then there is

   A) a decrease in a government budget deficit.
   B) an increase in a government budget surplus.
   C) a rightward shift in the demand for loanable funds.
   D) an upward movement along the loanable funds supply schedule.

4. In the classical loanable funds market, if there is a government budget deficit, the equilibrium real interest rate arises when

   I. the quantity of loanable funds demanded is equal to the quantity of loanable funds supplied.
   II. private investment plus the government budget deficit is equal to household saving.
   III. the equilibrium nominal interest rate is just equal to the expected inflation rate.

   A) I only
   B) III only
   C) both I and II
   D) both II and III

5. If the government's budget is balanced and households decide to increase their saving at any given real interest rate, then according to classical theory there will be

   I. an increase in the supply of loanable funds.
   II. a rise in the equilibrium real interest rate.
   III. an increase in equilibrium investment.

   A) I only
   B) II only
   C) both I and III
   D) both II and III

6. If the government's budget is balanced and businesses decide to reduce their investment spending at any given real interest rate, then according to classical t theory there will be

   I. a decrease in the supply of loanable funds.
   II. a fall in the equilibrium real interest rate.
   III. a decrease in equilibrium saving.

   A) I only
   B) II only
   C) both I and III
   D) both II and III

7. According to the classical model, a rise in government spending not matched by a tax increase would cause

   I. a rise in aggregate demand for goods and services.
   II. a reduction in private investment spending.
   III. a reduction in the government's deficit.

   A) I only
   B) II only
   C) both I and III
   D) both II and III

8. According to the classical model, a tax cut not matched by a reduction in government expenditures would cause

   I. a rise in the equilibrium real interest rate.
   II. an increase in the government's budget deficit.
   III. a rise in aggregate demand for goods and services.

   A) I only
   B) III only
   C) both I and II
   D) both II and III

9. The classical theory of nominal interest rate determination indicates that if expected inflation is unchanged, an increase in the nominal interest rate can result from

   A) a reduction in the expected growth rate in the quantity of money in circulation.
   B) an increase in government spending not matched by an increase in taxes.
   C) an increase in taxes not matched by an increase in government spending.
   D) an increased desire of individuals to save at any given real interest rate.

10. The classical theory of nominal interest rate determination indicates that a reduction in the nominal interest rate can result from

    A) a reduction in the expected growth rate in the quantity of money in circulation.
    B) an increase in government spending not matched by an increase in taxes.
    C) a reduction in taxes not matched by a decrease in government spending.
    D) an increased desire of firms to invest at any given real interest rate.

11. If there is an increase in the rate of growth in the quantity of money, then if all other factors in the classical model are unchanged,

    I. there is an increase in the expected rate of inflation.
    II. there is an increase in the nominal interest rate.
    III. the equilibrium real interest rate is unaffected.

    A) both I and II only
    B) both I and III only
    C) both II and III only
    D) I, II, and III

Classical Macroeconomic Theory — Interest Rates and Exchange Rates

12. If there is an decrease in the rate of growth in the quantity of money, then if all other factors in the classical model are unchanged,

   I. there is a decrease in the expected rate of inflation.
   II. there is an decrease in the real interest rate.
   III. the equilibrium nominal interest rate rises.

   A) I only
   B) III only
   C) both I and II
   D) both II and III

13. Under purchasing power parity, a nation's exchange rate, measured in terms of units of domestic currency per unit of foreign currency, is equal to

   A) the domestic price level divided by the foreign price level.
   B) the foreign price level divided by the domestic price level.
   C) the foreign price level times the domestic price level.
   D) the domestic price level times the real interest rate.

14. Under purchasing power parity, at the equilibrium exchange rate, expressed in terms of units of domestic currency per unit of foreign currency, the domestic price level is equal to

   A) the foreign price level times the exchange rate.
   B) the foreign price level divided by the exchange rate.
   C) the foreign quantity of money in circulation times the exchange rate.
   D) the foreign quantity of money in circulation divided by the exchange rate.

15. In the classical model, a rise in the foreign price level would, if other factors are unchanged, cause

   A) a depreciation of the domestic currency.
   B) an appreciation of the domestic currency.
   C) a rise in the domestic nation's real interest rate.
   D) a fall in the domestic nation's real interest rate.

16. According to the classical model, if a nation were to experience a technological improvement, then if all other factors are unchanged,

   A) the foreign price level would decline.
   B) the foreign price level would increase.
   C) the domestic nation's currency would appreciate.
   D) the domestic nation's currency would depreciate.

17. According to the classical model, if a nation's central bank were to unexpectedly increase the quantity of money in circulation, then if all other factors were unchanged,

   A) real interest rates at home and abroad would increase.
   B) real interest rates at home and abroad would decline.
   C) the domestic nation's currency would appreciate.
   D) the domestic nation's currency would depreciate.

18. If there is a sudden influx of foreign immigrants seeking domestic employment, the classical model's prediction is that the domestic price level will _____, thereby inducing a _____.

   A) increase; foreign currency depreciation
   B) decrease; foreign currency appreciation
   C) increase; domestic currency depreciation
   D) decrease; domestic currency appreciation

19. If domestic firms expand their capital resources, the classical model's prediction is that the domestic price level will _____, thereby inducing a _____.

   A) increase; foreign currency appreciation
   B) decrease; foreign currency depreciation
   C) increase; domestic currency appreciation
   D) decrease; domestic currency depreciation

20. If the domestic income velocity of money increases, the classical model's prediction is that the domestic price level will _____, thereby inducing a _____.

   A) decrease; domestic currency depreciation
   B) increase; domestic currency appreciation
   C) decrease; foreign currency depreciation
   D) increase; foreign currency appreciation

Short-Answer Questions

1. What is the real interest rate?

2. Why does the loanable funds supply schedule slope upward?

3. Why does the loanable funds demand schedule slope downward?

4. When does a government budget deficit exist?

5. When does a government budget surplus exist?

6. If an increase in the government's deficit causes a rise in the real interest rate that induces declines in private investment and consumption spending, what has occurred?

7. Why is there complete crowding out in the classical model?

8. In the classical model, monetary policy actions cannot affect the real interest rate, so how can an increase in the rate of growth of the amount of money in circulation affect the nominal interest rate?

9. Under purchasing power parity, how can we compute the rate of exchange of a home nation's currency relative to the currency of a foreign nation?

10. What is an open economy?

Chapter 5: Utopia Just Beyond the Horizon, or Future Shock? — The Theory of Economic Growth

Chapter Summary

Economists use the annual rate of change in per capita real GDP as their key measure of economic growth. There are problems entailed in relying on this measure of growth, because it does not account for changes in the quality of goods and services, sometimes fails to reflect improvements in living standards, does not indicate that all of a nation's residents truly benefit from growth, and does not take into account intergenerational externalities stemming from growth. Nonetheless, most economists concur that it is the best available measure of how much the real income of a nation's average resident grows from year to year.

Although growth rates in per capita real GDP usually differ by just a few percentage points or even by just tenths of percentage points, small differences in growth rates among nations' growth rates can produce differences in future per capita output levels. This is so because growth has a cumulative, or compound, effect over a number of years. Although a number of developing nations have experienced rapid growth in recent years, industrialized nations in Europe, Japan, and the United States experienced have experienced declines in rates of economic growth since the 1980s. Because of the compounding effect of economic growth, reduced growth rates during the past two decades in these nations ultimately will lead to significantly smaller per capita incomes than the nations otherwise might have hoped to attain.

There are three key determinants of annual economic growth. One of these is the proportionate rise in output caused by growth in labor employment during a year. A second determinant is the proportionate increase in output induced by growth in the amount of capital during a year. The third growth determinant is the annual proportionate rise in productivity, or the change in productivity during a year relative to total productivity.

Given a fixed population, increased labor force participation leads to higher employment of labor and increased real GDP, which raises a nation's rate of economic growth. Population growth increases the number of workers, which spurs growth in aggregate real GDP but which also raises the number of people into which real GDP is divided to compute per capita GDP. Thus, the effect of population growth on economic growth is ambiguous. Recent research indicates that population growth is more likely to push up economic growth in nations whose residents have more economic freedom. Most evidence indicates that immigration has spurred economic growth in the United States, although the growth effects of immigration remain debatable.

As shown in Figure 5, higher labor productivity enhances economic growth. An increase in the marginal product of labor causes increases in the equilibrium real wage and employment level, as depicted in panels (a) and (b). In addition, a rise in the marginal product of labor steepens the aggregate production function, as shown in panel (c). Thus, increased labor productivity has a two-fold effect on real output, inducing two rightward shifts in the aggregate supply schedule in panel (d). In recent years, however, labor productivity in the United States and other developed nations has leveled off, which has contributed to a flattening of economic growth rates in these countries.

Figure 5: Labor Productivity and Real Output Growth

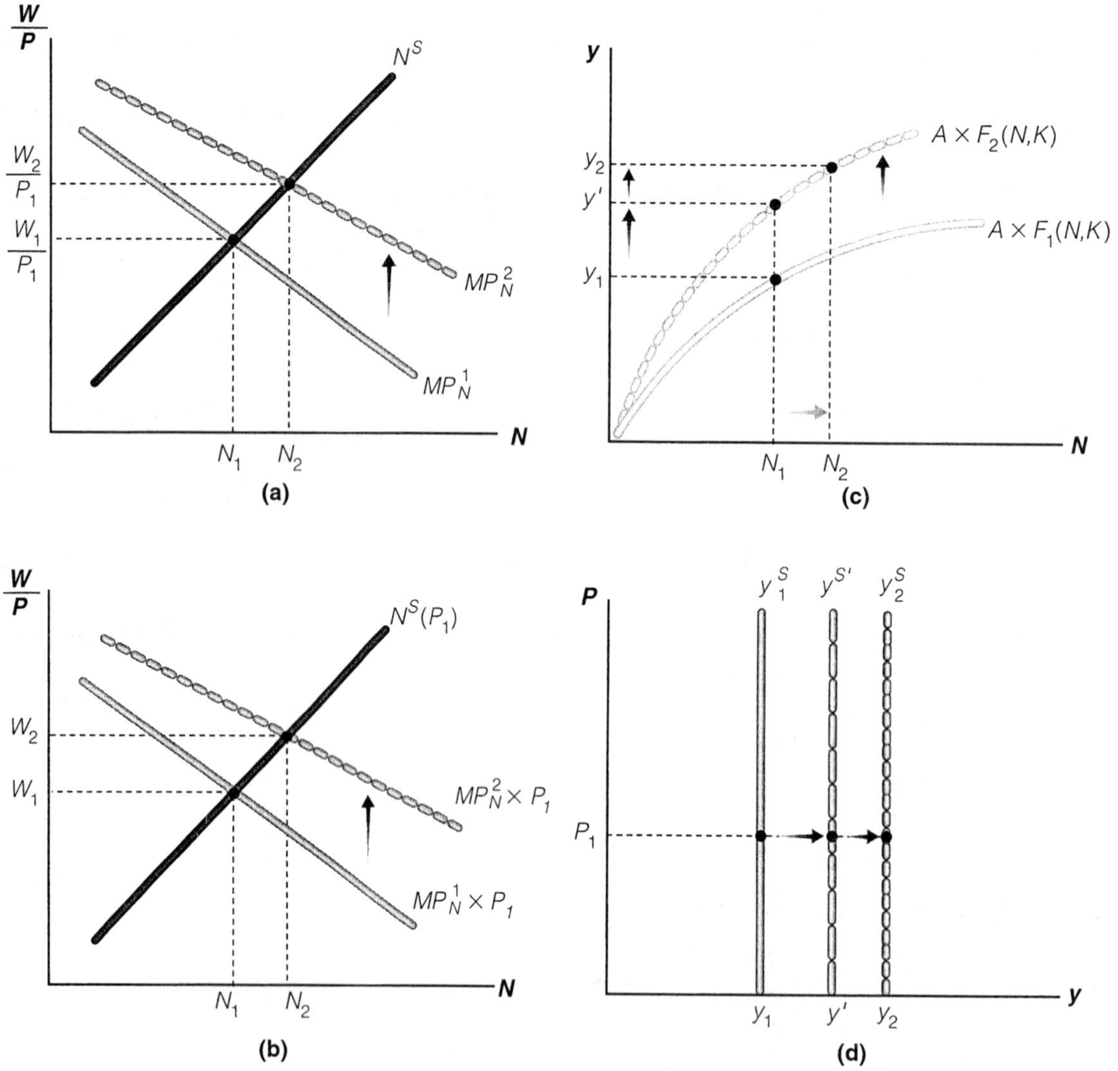

Countries accumulate new capital by postponing consumption and making capital investments. Businesses add to their use of capital by investing to the point at which the marginal product of capital is equal to the real interest rate. As a result, increased national saving, a fall in the real interest rate, or a rise in the productivity of capital lead to a rise in capital accumulation and greater near-term, if not long-term, economic growth.

The new growth theory highlights productivity growth as a determinant of growth in per capital GDP. Adherents of the new growth theory argue that investments in human capital, acquisition and use of knowledge and knowledge-enhancing technologies, are fundamental means of raising rates of long-term economic growth. Such investments, they contend, spur additional investment, thereby making economic growth a self-perpetuating process.

In the past, many have argued that protecting home industries from foreign competition can advance a nation's economic growth. Most economists today, including new growth theorists, contend that protectionism retards the global spread of new ideas and technologies, so that net effect of protectionism on economic growth can be negative. Experience with protectionism appears to offer some support for this contrary view.

Key Terms and Concepts

Capital
Complements in production
Compounded growth
Compound growth rate
Depreciation
Economic growth
Economies of scale
Gross investment
Human capital
Innovation
Intergenerational externalities
Marginal product of capital (MP_K)

Net investment
New growth theory
Protectionism
Quotas
Substitutes in production
Supply-side economics
Tariffs

Multiple-Choice Questions

1. The key measure of economic growth is the rate of growth of

    A) the consumer price index.
    B) the capital stock.
    C) per capita GDP.
    D) employment.

2. Suppose that during 2005, state A, which has 5 million residents, produces a level of real GDP equal to $20,000 million, while state B, with 2 million residents, produces $10,000 million in real GDP. In 2010, population levels in both states remain unchanged, but real GDP rises to $25,000 million in the more populous state and to $12,000 million in the less populous state. Which of the following statements is correct?

    I. In 2005, state B has higher per capita GDP as compared with state A.
    II. In 2010, state A has higher per capital GDP as compared with state B.
    III. Between 2005 and 2010, the rate of growth of per capita output was higher in state B as compared with state A.

    A) I only
    B) III only
    C) both I and III
    D) both II and III

3. Which of the following is not a problem that arises in comparing per capita GDP levels of two different nations?

    A) differences in the distribution of GDP among the nations' residents
    B) different degrees of quality of the nations' goods and services
    C) different approaches to tabulating GDP in the two nations
    D) different populations in the two countries

4. Because growth compounds across years, if a relatively poor nation's per capita-GDP growth rate exceeds that of a relatively wealthy nation by the same small amount every year, then

   A) after the passage of a sufficient number of years, the initially poor nation's per capita GDP ultimately will surpass that of the initially wealthy nation.
   B) the relatively wealthy nation's per capita GDP will grow at a compound rate that causes its real GDP to outstrip that of the poorer nation.
   C) after the passage of a sufficient number of years, the relatively poor nation's per capita GDP must decline by to an even lower level.
   D) the relatively poor nation's per capita GDP will rise over time, but it will always lag slightly behind that of the more wealthy nation.

5. An example of an intergenerational externality arising from economic growth would be

   A) the burial of PCB-laden electronic capacitors during the personal-computer boom of the 1980s and 1990s that results in ground-water contamination that appears after 2010.
   B) an accident at a nuclear power plant, which previously had provided power for new factories, that forces the immediate evacuation of residents within a 100-square-mile area.
   C) the ability of consumers in the early twenty-first century to consume a larger number of goods and services because of significant economic growth during the 1980s and 1990s.
   D) the creation of new communities around research facilities that stimulates the immediate migration into those communities from surrounding cities and states.

6. The three key determinants of economic growth are

   A) the rates of growth of output demand, of consumption productivity, and of the average ratio of saving to income.
   B) the rates of growth of labor and capital productivity, of the labor force, and of the stock of capital goods.
   C) the rates of growth of financial-market transactions, of stock-market activity, and of money payments.
   D) the rates of growth of exports, of imports, and of foreign exchange transactions.

7. As compared with the period between the 1940s and the 1970s, since the 1980s the world's industrialized nations experienced

   A) higher negative rates of per capita GDP growth.
   B) higher positive rates of per capita GDP growth.
   C) lower negative rates of per capita GDP growth.
   D) lower positive rates of per capita GDP growth.

8. Which statement about the effects of immigration on economic growth is correct?

   A) Immigration has two self-reinforcing effects: It raises measured per capita growth by increasing the labor force and, thus output, and the resulting increases in output spur further immigration and labor-force and output growth.
   B) Immigration has two conflicting effects: It reduces measured per capita growth by increasing the denominator in computing GDP per capita while it raises measured per capita growth by increasing the labor force and, thus, output.
   C) Immigration unambiguously reduces output growth by increasing the population and reducing per capita GDP.
   D) Immigration unambiguously raises output growth by increasing the population and the labor force.

9. According to recent research,

   A) greater economic freedom unambiguously fuels economic growth, but greater political freedom has the potential to retard economic growth somewhat.
   B) greater political freedom unambiguously fuels economic growth, but greater economic freedom has the potential to retard economic growth somewhat.
   C) greater political and economic freedom both have the potential to retard economic growth somewhat.
   D) greater political and economic freedom both unambiguously fuel economic growth.

10. The additional output that can be produced by the addition of one more unit of capital is the

    A) saving rate.
    B) economic growth rate.
    C) marginal product of capital.
    D) average rate of real investment.

11. Which of the following would definitely result from an increase in labor productivity that results in a rise in additional output from each additional unit of labor?

    I. an increase in labor force participation
    II. an increase in the demand for labor
    III. an increase in employment

    A) I only
    B) III only
    C) both I and III
    D) both II and III

12. Which of the following would result from a decline in the real interest rate?

    I. an increase in the use of capital goods by firms
    II. an increase in firm investment
    III. a rise in household saving

    A) I only
    B) III only
    C) both I and II
    D) both II and III

13. Which of the following would definitely follow from an increase in capital productivity that results in a rise in additional output from each additional unit of capital?

    I. a decline in the real interest rate
    II. an increase in firm investment
    III. a fall in household saving

    A) I only
    B) II only
    C) both I and III
    D) both II and III

14. The transformation of a new process or product into a means of lowering production costs or new goods and services in the marketplace is called

    A) invention.
    B) innovation.
    C) economic growth.
    D) capital accumulation.

15. If capital and labor are complements in production, then

    A) an increased use of capital goods leads to a rise in the use of labor.
    B) an increased use of capital goods leads to a decline in the use of labor.
    C) capital accumulation occurs at a faster rate than the growth of labor force participation.
    D) labor force participation grows at a faster rate than the rate of capital accumulation.

16. Which of the following could lead to simultaneous increases in the use of both capital and labor?

    I. economies of scale in production
    II. substitutability of capital and labor in production
    III. complementarity of capital and labor in production

    A) I only
    B) II only
    C) both I and III
    D) both II and III

17. According to the new growth theory,

    I. greater investment in knowledge causes a once-and-for-all increase in GDP.
    II. economic growth can be a self-perpetuating process.
    III. investment in human capital is crucial to growth.

    A) I only
    B) III only
    C) both I and II
    D) both II and III

18. Human capital refers to

    A) robot forms of capital.
    B) capital goods that complement labor.
    C) capital goods that substitute for labor.
    D) knowledge and skills of the labor force.

19. Protectionism refers to policies intended to

    A) prevent substitutions of labor with capital.
    B) hinder flows of goods and services from abroad.
    C) hinder the development of new processes and products.
    D) prevent the diffusion of knowledge across the labor force.

20. Which of the following is a common means of implementing protectionism?

    A) imposing high tariffs
    B) inhibiting national saving
    C) maintaining high real interest rates
    D) inducing a low marginal product of capital

Short-Answer Questions

1. What is a compound growth rate?

2. How do economists calculate a nation's per capita real GDP?

3. How does increased labor force participation raise per capita real GDP?

4. What group of economists advocates policies that encourage labor force participation, such as low tax rates on wage income, as a means of increasing per capita real GDP?

5. What is the difference between gross investment and net investment?

6. What is the term for an inflow of new residents from another nation?

7. What causes an upward rotation of the aggregate production function?

8. What is the term for a net accumulation of new capital?

9. What do economists call the knowledge and skills of people in the labor force?

10. What is a numerical limit on cross-border shipments of goods and services?

Chapter 6: Business Cycles and Short-Run Macroeconomics — Essentials of the Keynesian System

Chapter Summary

Business cycles are variations in aggregate real income relative to natural GDP, or the level of real GDP consistent with the economy's long-run growth path. An economy in a phase in the business cycle called a recession when real GDP declines. The low point of a recession, when actual real GDP is at its lowest point relative to its natural path is the trough of the business cycle. A particularly deep trough and long-lasting recession constitute a depression, such as the depression occurred in the United States during the 1930s. A rise in real GDP occurs during an expansion phase of the business cycle. The business cycle reaches a peak at a point at which actual real GDP rises to its highest point relative to natural GDP during the cycle.

The unemployment rate, is the percentage of the civilian labor force—all individuals of working age who are not in the military or confined to an institution such as a hospital and who either have a job or are actively seeking a job—who are not working yet are available for and actively seeking a job. Those who are unemployed fall into three categories. One is frictional unemployment, or the portion of the labor force consisting of people who are qualified for gainful employment but who are not working temporarily, perhaps because they recently quit a job to take another that will start within a few weeks. The second category is structural unemployment, which is the portion of the civilian labor force made up of people who would like to be gainfully employed but who lack skills and other attributes necessary to obtain a job. Economists call the ratio of those who are frictionally and structurally unemployed to the civilian labor force the natural rate of unemployment, or the unemployment rate that would arise if the economy could stay on its long-run growth path.

A traditional focus of Keynesian macroeconomic theory has been placed on the third category of unemployment is cyclical unemployment, which is the portion of the civilian labor force composed of those who lose their jobs because of business-cycle fluctuations. John Maynard Keynes, the twentieth-century economist for whom this approach is named, rejected certain central features of classical theory in favor of a theory that might be able to explain the causes of short-run business cycles. Among other things, the theory that he proposed relied on alternative views of labor supply, money demand, and consumption and investment expenditures. As compared with the classical model, the theory also focused more narrowly on the short run.

The starting point of the basic Keynesian model is the circular flow of income and expenditures. This flow implies two key identities, or truisms. One, called the income identity, states that real income must, by definition, equal the sum of real consumption (c), real saving (s), real net taxes (t), and real imports (im), or $y \equiv c + s + t + im$. The other, called the product identity, states that real income must equal total real expenditures on output, which equal the sum of real consumption, real realized investment (i_r), real government expenditures (g), and real exports (x), or $y \equiv c + i_r + g + x$.

Keynesian theory seeks to explain movements in these various components of total income and expenditures. The theory proposes that the amount of real saving, real import expenditures, and real consumption spending depends positively upon real disposable income, $y_d \equiv y - t$. From the income identity, disposable income is equal to $y_d \equiv c + s + im$, and so a change in disposable income must equal $\Delta y_d \equiv \Delta c + \Delta s + \Delta im$. This, in turn, implies that $\Delta y_d / \Delta y_d = 1 \equiv \Delta c / \Delta y_d + \Delta s / \Delta y_d + \Delta im / \Delta y_d$. The first ratio on the right side of this identity, $\Delta c / \Delta y_d$, is the marginal propensity to consume (*MPC*) , or the change in real consumption that is induced by a change in real disposable income. The second ratio, $\Delta s / \Delta y_d$, is the marginal propensity to save (*MPS*), which is a change in real saving caused by a change in real disposable income. The third ratio, $\Delta im / \Delta y_d$ is the marginal propensity to import (*MPIM*). Hence, all three marginal propensities must sum to one.

In the basic Keynesian model, we consider straight-line saving, import, and consumption functions, given by $s = -s_0 + (MPS \times y_d)$, $im = im_0 + (MPIM \times y_d)$, and $c = (s_0 - im_0) + [(1 - MPS - MPIM) \times y_d]$, respectively. The terms $-s_0$, im_0, and $(s_0 - im_0)$ represent autonomous saving, autonomous imports, and autonomous consumption, or the amounts of saving, import spending, and consumption expenditures that would occur irrespective of the current level of disposable income y_d. The terms *MPS*, *MPIM*, and $(1 - MPS - MPIM) = MPC$ are the slopes of the saving, import, and consumption functions, and they are equal to the marginal propensity to save, the marginal propensity to import, and the marginal propensity to consume, respectively.

The basic Keynesian theory also proposes investment, government spending, net tax, and export functions. The Keynesian theory of investment expenditures stems from the classical theory of investment. Domestic desired investment depends negatively on the real interest rate, or the nominal interest rate minus the expected inflation rate. Thus, a decline in the real interest rate causes desired real investment spending to rise, implying that the desired investment schedule slopes downward. A rise in desired investment could also occur because of a rightward shift in the desired investment schedule, perhaps because of a general anticipation by firms of higher profits in the future. In the basic Keynesian model, desired investment, government expenditures and net taxes are autonomous, or unrelated to real income. Real exports also are unrelated to domestic real income, although changes in the real incomes of foreign residents or variations in exchange rates can influence real exports.

Total spending on domestically produced goods and services is the sum of household consumption spending, desired investment spending, government expenditures, and spending on domestic exports by residents of foreign nations, or $c + i + g + x$. Summing the consumption function and autonomous investment, government spending, and exports yields an upward-sloping aggregate expenditures schedule that indicates the combined desired spending of households, firms, the government, and foreign residents on domestically produced output at any given level of domestic real income y. The vertical intercept of this schedule is aggregate net autonomous expenditures, which is the total net amount of spending on domestically produced output that is independent of the current level of total real income, and the slope of the aggregate expenditures schedule is equal to the consumption function's slope, or the marginal propensity to consume, $MPC = 1 - MPS - MPIM$.

The equilibrium flow of real income is the single level of income at which households, firms, the government, and foreign residents desire to purchase all real output that is produced and sold by domestic firms. This implies that equilibrium real income is the real income level at which the real value of domestically produced output, or real income, is equal to aggregate desired expenditures are equal to the real value of domestically produced output, or $y = c + i + g + x$. This income level is achieved at the point at which the aggregate expenditures schedule crosses the 45-degree line, along which real income along the horizontal axis is equal to the level of aggregate desired expenditures along the vertical axis. The leakages-injections approach to determining equilibrium real income yields the same real income level, at which all leakages from the domestic flow of spending, which are saving, net taxes, and imports, ultimately are reinjected back into that flow via investment spending, government expenditures, and exports, so that $s + t + im = i + g + x$.

A key implication of the basic Keynesian model of real income determination is the multiplier effect, or the fact that a given 1-unit change in aggregate net autonomous expenditures, which is a 1-unit movement in the intercept of the aggregate desired expenditures schedule, causes a greater-than-1-unit change in equilibrium real income in the same direction. The ratio $1 / (MPS + MPIM) = 1 / (1 - MPC)$ is the Keynesian autonomous expenditures multiplier. This multiplier measures the size of the multiplier effect on equilibrium real income (Δy) resulting in an increase in the level of autonomous net aggregate expenditures, such as the movement from the schedule $c + i + g + x$ to the schedule $(c + i + g + x)'$ in Figure 6.

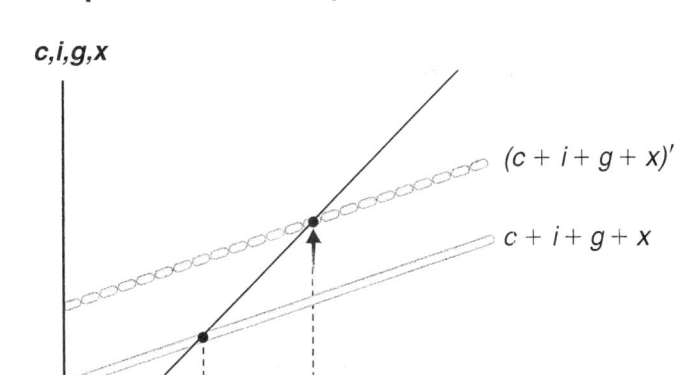

Figure 6: The Effect of a Rise in Autonomous Net Aggregate Expenditures on Equilibrium Real Income

In the Keynesian theory, business cycles result from variations in autonomous net aggregate expenditures that cause equilibrium real income to differ from its long-run, natural level. A recessionary gap in spending arises in a situation in which equilibrium real income is below its natural level, so that aggregate desired expenditures would need to increase to move equilibrium real income back toward the level consistent with the economy's long-run growth path. An inflationary gap takes place when equilibrium real income exceeds its natural level, so that there is an excess amount of real aggregate desired expenditures relative to the amount necessary to keep the economy at its natural income level. Keynes argues that fiscal policy actions—variations in autonomous government spending and net taxes—could, via the multiplier effect, stabilize equilibrium real income at its natural level, thereby eliminating recessionary and inflationary gaps and smoothing business cycles. Thus, Keynes promoted countercyclical fiscal policies, or increases in government spending and tax cuts during recessions and reductions in government spending and tax increases during expansions.

The balance of trade is equal to exports minus imports, or *x - im*. Because imports increase with a rise in disposable income, the trade balance schedule slopes downward. The equilibrium trade balance is the balance of trade that arises at an economy's current equilibrium real income level.

Key Terms and Concepts

Aggregate net autonomous expenditures
Aggregate expenditures schedule
Autonomous consumption
Autonomous expenditures multiplier
Autonomous investment
Average propensity to consume (*APC*)
Average propensity to save (*APS*)
Countercyclical fiscal policy
Cyclical unemployment
Depression
Expansion
45-degree line
Frictional unemployment
Income identity
Inflationary gap
Marginal propensity to consume (*MPC*)
Marginal propensity to import (*MPIM*)
Marginal propensity to save (*MPS*)
Multiplier effect
Natural GDP
Natural rate of unemployment
Peak
Product identity
Real consumption
Real disposable income
Real export spending
Real household saving
Real imports
Real net taxes
Real realized investment

Recessionary gap
Recession
Structural unemployment
Transfer payments
Trough
Unemployment rate

Multiple-Choice Questions

1. The level of real GDP along a long-run growth path that a nation's economy would tend to follow in the absence of cyclical fluctuations is called

    A) cyclical GDP.
    B) natural GDP.
    C) potential GDP.
    D) full-employment GDP.

2. If during the current business cycle real GDP is farthest below the long-run growth path that it would have followed in the absence of cyclical variations, then the economy must be

    A) at the trough of a business cycle.
    B) at the peak of a business cycle.
    C) experiencing an expansion.
    D) in a depression period.

3. For purposes of computing the unemployment rate, which of the following individuals would be included in the civilian labor force?

    I. a 14-year-old high school student who babysits part-time
    II. a laid-off 21-year-old factory worker who is looking for a new job
    III. a 29-year-old Army captain stationed at a U.S. base

    A) I only
    B) II only
    C) both I and III
    D) both II and III

4. For purposes of computing the unemployment rate, which of the following individuals would be included among the ranks of the unemployed?

   I. a 28-year-old with a Ph.D. in Russian literature who has given up hope of finding a job and hence has stopped searching.
   II. a 17-year-old high school student searching unsuccessfully for a job.
   III. a laid-off 21-year-old factory worker who is looking for a new job.

   A) I only
   B) II only
   C) both I and III
   D) both II and III

5. Which of the following are included in the natural rate of unemployment?

   I. structural unemployment
   II. frictional unemployment
   III. cyclical unemployment

   A) both I and II only
   B) both I and III only
   C) both II and III only
   D) I, II, and III

6. Frictional unemployment includes individuals who are part of the civilian labor force and who

   A) are qualified for gainful employment but who recently quit a job because they have accepted another job that they will begin at a later time.
   B) would like to be gainfully employed but who lack skills and other attributes necessary to obtain a job.
   C) have lost their jobs because of personality conflicts with their supervisors.
   D) have lost their jobs because of a business-cycle downturn.

7. According to the income identity from the circular flow,

   A) the value of real income equals the value of real output.
   B) leakages from the flow of spending must equal reinjections into that flow.
   C) real income must, by definition, equal the sum of real consumption, real saving, real net taxes, and real imports.
   D) real income must, by definition, equal the sum of real consumption, real realized investment, real government spending, and real exports.

Business Cycles and Short-Run Macroeconomics — Essentials of the Keynesian System 57

8. Which of the following is true of the marginal propensity to consume (MPC)?

   I. The MPC is equal to a change in consumption resulting from a change in disposable income.
   II. To compute the MPC, we can divide the amount of real consumption by the level of real disposable income.
   III. To compute the MPC, we can subtract the marginal propensity to save and the marginal propensity to import from one.

   A) I only
   B) II only
   C) both I and III
   D) both II and III

9. Which of the following is true of the marginal propensity to import (MPIM)?

   I. The MPIM is the slope of the import function.
   II. To compute the MPIM, we can divide the amount of real imports by the level of real disposable income.
   III. To compute the MPIM, we can add together the marginal propensity to save and the marginal propensity to consume.

   A) I only
   B) II only
   C) both I and III
   D) both II and III

10. If autonomous saving is equal to $10 billion and if the marginal propensity to save is equal to 0.2, then if real disposable income is equal to $40 billion, then the amount of real saving is equal to

    A) $5 billion.
    B) $18 billion.
    C) $45 billion.
    D) $50 billion.

11. At the equilibrium level of real income,

    I. Leakages from the flow of real spending equal reinjections into that flow.
    II. Desired real investment spending is equal to realized real investment spending.
    III. Real income is equal to the sum of real consumption, desired real investment spending, real government spending, and real exports.

    A) both I and II only
    B) both I and III only
    C) both II and III only
    D) I, II, and III

12. If the marginal propensity to import is equal to 0.07 and the marginal propensity to save is equal to 0.13, then

    A) the marginal propensity to consume is equal to 0.06, and the autonomous expenditures multiplier is equal to 1/(0.06) = 16.7.
    B) the marginal propensity to consume is equal to 0.20, and the autonomous expenditures multiplier is equal to 1/(0.20) = 5.0.
    C) the marginal propensity to consume is equal to 0.80, and the autonomous expenditures multiplier is equal to 1/(0.80) = 1.25.
    D) the marginal propensity to consume is equal to 0.80, and the autonomous expenditures multiplier is equal to 1/(0.20) = 5.0.

13. If the autonomous expenditures multiplier is equal to 3.0, the marginal propensity to consume is equal to two-thirds, and the marginal propensity to import is equal to one-sixth, then the marginal propensity to save must be equal to

    A) one-sixth.
    B) one-third.
    C) two-thirds.
    D) one.

14. If the economy experiences a recessionary gap, then which of the following policy actions might, at least in theory, help to reduce or eliminate the recessionary gap?

    I. an increase in lump-sum taxes
    II. an increase in government spending
    III. a policy intended to eliminate a trade deficit by spurring exports

    A) I only
    B) III only
    C) both I and II
    D) both II and III

15. Suppose that the current equilibrium level of real income is equal to $11,000 billion. The long-run, potential level of real income desired by society, however, is equal to $12,000 billion. The marginal propensity to consume is equal to 0.75. It follows that

   A) there is a recessionary gap that could be eliminated by a government spending reduction of $1,000 billion.
   B) there is an inflationary gap that could be eliminated by a government spending reduction of $250 billion.
   C) there is a recessionary gap that could be eliminated by a lump-sum tax reduction of $333.3 billion.
   D) there is an inflationary gap that could be eliminated by a lump-sum tax increase of $250 billion.

16. If the current level of real income is equal to $11,500 billion, and if the equilibrium level of real income is equal to $12,000 billion, then

   A) there is an inflationary gap of $500 billion.
   B) there is a recessionary gap of $500 billion.
   C) businesses would begin to accumulate undesired inventories of finished goods.
   D) businesses would begin to experience undesired reductions in inventories of finished goods.

17. In principle, which of the following could result from a decline in equilibrium real income caused by a fall in autonomous investment spending?

   I. a trade surplus
   II. a recessionary gap
   III. a fall in autonomous consumption

   A) I only
   B) III only
   C) both I and II
   D) both II and III

18. By definition, at the equilibrium level of real income,

   A) the trade balance is equal to zero.
   B) business inventories are equal to zero.
   C) real income is equal to real household consumption.
   D) real income is equal to aggregate desired real expenditures.

19. If the equilibrium trade balance is equal to zero, then which of the following must be true?

    A) Leakages from the spending flow exceed reinjections into that flow.
    B) Real export spending is equal to real import spending.
    C) Real income exceeds aggregate desired spending.
    D) Businesses accumulate undesired inventories.

20. If there is currently a trade deficit at the current equilibrium real income level, then if all other factors are unchanged, which of the following policy actions would tend to reduce the trade deficit?

    A) a rise in government spending
    B) enactment of an increase in net taxes
    C) a reduction in subsidies paid to exporters
    D) an increase in the government's budget deficit

Short-Answer Questions

1. What is the term for a period in which real GDP fluctuates above and below its natural growth path?

2. What is a deep, long-lasting recession?

3. By definition, what is the unemployment rate?

4. What are transfer payments?

5. What is the average propensity to import?

6. What is autonomous consumption?

7. What two factors influence spending on a nation's exports?

8. What is the product identity?

9. How does an inflationary gap occur?

10. Holding all other factors unchanged, what is the effect on the equilibrium trade balance if equilibrium real income rises?

Chapter 7: A Meaningful Role for Government — Fiscal Policy in the Traditional Keynesian System

Chapter Summary

About 90 percent of taxes actually collected by the U.S. government stem from three basic types of income taxes: personal income taxes, corporate income taxes, and social insurance payroll taxes. The U.S. income tax system is designed to be a progressive income tax system in which the amount of income taxes assessed is a higher percentage of income for higher-income individuals. In contrast, in a regressive income tax system, the amount of income taxes assessed is a lower percentage of income for higher-income individuals. A proportional income tax system is one in individuals in any income classification pays remains a constant percentage of their incomes in taxes. In a proportional income tax system, the marginal income tax rate, which is a change in income taxes paid for a given increase in income, equals the average tax rate, which is the ratio of total tax payments to total income. By way of contrast, in progressive or regressive income tax systems, the marginal and average income tax rates differ at various income levels.

In the simplifying case of a proportional income tax system, we can modify the basic Keynesian model by using the tax function, $t = t_0 + \tau y$, in which the first component t_0 includes tax revenues from sources other than the income tax, net of any transfer payments and the second component represents income tax revenues, where the marginal tax rate is τ. On a diagram, t_0 denotes net autonomous taxes and is the vertical intercept of the tax function. The slope of the function, $\Delta t/\Delta y$, is the overall marginal tax rate, which does not necessarily equal to overall average tax rate, which is equal to $t/y = t_0/y + \tau$.

With this tax function, the slope of the consumption function is equal one minus the marginal tax rate times the *MPC*. On the one hand, an increase in the income tax rate reduces the slope of the consumption function, which, as shown in Figure 7, rotates the aggregate desired expenditures schedule downward and reduces equilibrium real income. On the other hand, with this tax function the size of the autonomous expenditures multiplier depends on the income tax rate τ. An increase in the income tax rate raises the denominator of the multiplier, thereby reducing the magnitude of the multiplier. Hence, a higher income tax rate reduces the size of the autonomous expenditures multiplier and makes equilibrium real income more stable in the face of changes in aggregate net autonomous expenditures. In this way, the income tax system functions as an automatic fiscal stabilizer.

Figure 7: The Effects of a Higher Marginal Income Tax Rate

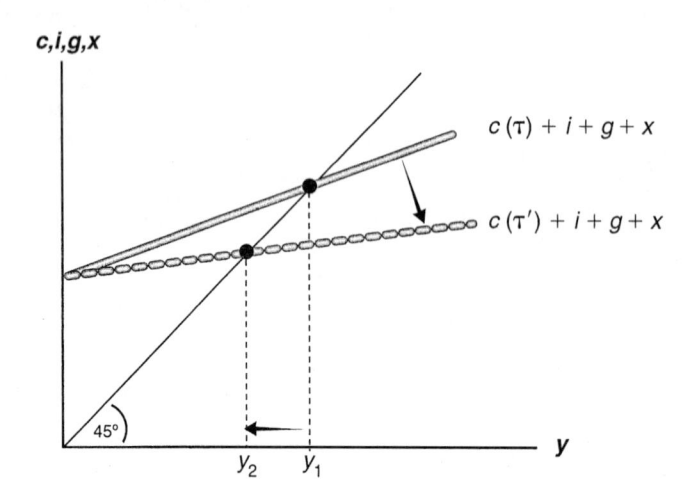

There are two views concerning the relationship between income tax rates and the government's income tax revenues. Under the purely static view, because tax revenues equal $t = t_0 + \tau y$, a reduction in the income tax rate causes a decline in total tax revenues. The dynamic view of the relationship, however, takes into account that a cut in the income tax rate also induces a rise in equilibrium real income. Consequently, along some sufficiently high range of income tax rates, a cut in the income tax rate actually would raise the government's income tax revenues.

In recent years some economists have questioned the extent to which tax changes actually can influence real consumption spending. Based on theorizing by the 18th-century economist David Ricardo, these economists have argued that a current tax cut implies a future tax increase that a government will have to enact to make interest payments on debt issued to finance the current tax cut. Consequently, individuals will allocate the current increase in disposable income owing to the tax cut to saving, from which they can draw to pay the higher future taxes. From this perspective, called the Ricardian equivalence proposition, a tax cut today effectively is the same as a tax increase in the future, and so current consumption and equilibrium real income are unaffected by a tax cut. In the modern version of this argument, proponents contend that individuals who care about the welfare of their children and grandchildren will recognize that current tax cuts will raise the tax burdens that future generations face. Therefore, they will pass savings from current tax cuts to their offspring via gifts or bequests, which are sums payable to their offspring following their deaths. Through such intergenerational transfers, a current older generation effectively will pay the addition tax burden that had falls on younger generations due to tax cuts granted to the older generation.

Factors that may weigh against the real-world relevance of the Ricardian equivalence proposition are (1) possible shortsightedness of current generations, (2) liquidity constraints that limit the availability of cash and credit to meet spending needs that people face at various points in their lives, (3) the imposition of most taxes through the application of tax rates to income, (4) self-interested motivations for bequests by older generations to younger generations, and (5) income uncertainty that older generations face, which can induce members of the older generation to respond to a tax cut by altering their consumption immediately rather than saving on behalf of younger generations.

Key Terms and Concepts

Automatic fiscal stabilizer
Average tax rate
Bequest
Intergenerational transfers
Laffer curve
Liquidity constraints
Marginal tax rate
Progressive tax system
Proportional tax system
Regressive tax system
Ricardian equivalence proposition

Multiple-Choice Questions

1. A proportional income tax system

   A) is regressive, meaning that lower-income people pay a larger portion of their income in taxes.
   B) is progressive, meaning that lower-income people pay a smaller portion of their income in taxes.
   C) is a system in which income is taxed at the same rate above a positive minimum level of income.
   D) is a system in which income is taxed at the same rate at every given level of income.

2. If an individual's income tax bill rises from $8,000 to $10,000 when her income rises from $80,000 to $90,000, then the marginal income tax rate over this income range is equal to

   A) $8,000 / $80,000 = 0.10 (10 percent).
   B) $10,000 / $90,000 = 0.111 (11.1 percent).
   C) $10,000 / $80,000 = 0.125 (12.5 percent).
   D) $2,000 / $10,000 = 0.20 (20 percent).

3. If an individual's income tax falls from $50,000 to $30,000 when his income falls from $150,000 to $120,000, then the marginal income tax rate over this income range is equal to

   A) $30,000 / $120,000 = 0.25 (25 percent).
   B) $50,000 / $150,000 = 0.33.3 (33.3 percent).
   C) $30,000 / $50,000 = 0.60 (60 percent).
   D) $20,000 / $30,000 = 0.667 (66.7 percent).

4. If an individual's income tax bill rises from $20,000 to $25,000 when her income rises from $100,000 to $125,000, then along this income range,

   I. the marginal tax rate and average tax rate both equal to 20 percent.
   II. the income tax system is progressive.
   III. the income tax system is regressive.

   A) I only
   B) III only
   C) both I and II
   D) both II and III

5. If a typical individual's income tax bill rises from $5,000 to $6,000 when his income rises from $50,000 to $60,000, then over this range of income, the tax system is

    A) regressive.
    B) progressive.
    C) proportional.
    D) autonomous.

6. If a typical individual's income tax bill remains unchanged at $20,000 when her income rises from $60,000 to $80,000, then over this range of income, the tax system is

    A) regressive.
    B) progressive.
    C) proportional.
    D) autonomous.

7. If a typical individual's income tax bill rises from $10,000 to $11,000 when his income rises from $30,000 to $44,000, then over this range of income, the tax system is

    A) regressive.
    B) progressive.
    C) proportional.
    D) autonomous.

8. In a proportional income tax system, an increase in the marginal tax rate

    A) steepens the tax function and makes the consumption function more shallowly sloped.
    B) makes the tax function more shallowly sloped and steepens the consumption function.
    C) makes both the tax function and the consumption function more shallowly sloped.
    D) steepens both the tax function and the consumption function.

9. In a proportional income tax system, a reduction in the marginal tax rate

   I. makes equilibrium real income less stable in the face of changes in autonomous investment.
   II. increases the size of the autonomous expenditures multiplier.
   III. shifts the consumption function upward.

   A) I only
   B) III only
   C) both I and II
   D) both II and III

10. The reason that the income tax system functions as an automatic fiscal stabilizer is that

    A) even as a decline in autonomous aggregate expenditures pushes equilibrium income downward, the accompanying rise in taxes reduces consumption spending.
    B) even as a decline in autonomous aggregate expenditures pushes equilibrium income downward, the accompanying fall in taxes boosts consumption spending.
    C) a tax increase pushes down autonomous aggregate expenditures and simultaneously induces an increase in consumption spending.
    D) a tax cut raises autonomous aggregate expenditures and simultaneously induces a reduction in consumption spending.

11. The reason that a higher income tax rate enhances the automatic-stabilizer property of a proportional income tax system is that when the tax rate is higher, a decline in income caused by a fall in autonomous spending induces a

    A) smaller reduction in taxes and hence a smaller increase in consumption.
    B) larger increase in taxes and hence a smaller reduction in consumption.
    C) smaller increase in taxes and hence a larger reduction in consumption.
    D) larger reduction in taxes and hence a larger increase in consumption.

12. According to the static view of the relationship between income tax rates and income tax revenues,

    A) income tax rates and income tax revenues are unrelated.
    B) an increase in the income tax rate always raises income tax revenues.
    C) an increase in the income tax rate leads to a rise in income tax revenues.
    D) an increase in the income tax rate makes equilibrium real income less stable.

13. According to the dynamic view of the relationship between income tax rates and income tax revenues,

    A) income tax rates and income tax revenues are unrelated.
    B) an increase in the income tax rate always raises income tax revenues.
    C) a decrease in the income tax rate may lead to a rise in income tax revenues.
    D) an increase in the income tax rate makes equilibrium real income less stable.

14. The Laffer curve illustrates

    I. an unambiguously direct relationship between income tax rates and revenues.
    II. the dynamic view of the relationship between income tax rates and revenues.
    III. the automatic fiscal stabilizer properties of the income tax system.

    A) I only
    B) II only
    C) both I and III
    D) both II and III

15. On a diagram with the income tax rate measured along the horizontal axis and the government's income tax revenues measured along the vertical axis, the static view of the relationship between income tax rates and revenues is illustrated by

    A) an inverted-U-shaped Laffer curve.
    B) a downward-sloping schedule.
    C) an upward-sloping schedule.
    D) a U-shaped Laffer curve.

16. A bequest is

    A) the current value of an amount of funds to be received at a future date.
    B) the future value of an amount of funds to be received in the present.
    C) an amount given to an heir upon one's death.
    D) a holiday gift to a friend or family member.

17. An intergenerational transfer is a sum of money that

    A) the entire population within a given age range chooses to redistribute among members of that same group based on who possesses the most wealth.
    B) the entire population within a given age range chooses to redistribute among members of that same group based on who pays the highest taxes.
    C) an individual within a certain age group gives or bequeaths to another individual within that age group.
    D) an individual within a certain age group gives or bequeaths to an individual who is part of a different age group.

18. An individual or household that is liquidity constrained responds to a current tax cut that creates a government budget deficit

    A) by saving the funds to have available to give to younger family members so that they can cover higher future taxes the government will impose to pay off the deficit.
    B) by saving the funds to have available to cover higher future taxes the government will impose to pay off the deficit.
    C) by using the funds to pay off existing individual or household debts.
    D) by using the funds to establish trust funds for future bequests.

19. Which of the following is consistent with the Ricardian equivalence proposition?

    I.   A tax increase causes no change in aggregate real consumption.
    II. A tax increase causes an increase in aggregate real saving.
    III. A tax increase induces a rise in real government spending.

    A) I only
    B) III only
    C) both I and II
    D) both II and III

20. Which of the following would be consistent with the Ricardian equivalence proposition?

    I.   A young couple struggling to make ends meet spends all the proceeds of a one-time tax cut.
    II. A parent gives a daughter funds to help pay her bills, including her taxes which recently increased.
    III. A grandmother bequeaths a sum of money to a grandson, who faces higher taxes than the grandmother faced during her lifetime.

    A) I only
    B) II only
    C) both I and III
    D) both II and III

Short-Answer Questions

1. What is the source of over 90 percent of the U.S. government's tax revenues?

2. What is the marginal income tax rate?

3. What is the average income tax rate?

4. What is a progressive income tax system?

5. What is a regressive income tax system?

6. How is the income tax system an automatic fiscal stabilizer?

7. What is the Laffer curve?

8. What is a bequest?

9. What is an intergenerational transfer?

10. What is the Ricardian equivalence hypothesis?

Chapter 8: Do Central Banks Matter? — Money in the Traditional Keynesian System

Chapter Summary

A key tenet of traditional Keynesian theory is that interactions among the interest rate, money, prices, and real income permit central banks to perform potentially important roles in smoothing business cycles within their nations' economies. A fundamental rationale for this potential stabilizing role for central banks is Keynes's theory of the demand for money. Keynes proposed three reasons, or motives, for people to hold money. The first of these is the transactions motive, which is the incentive to hold money for use in planned transactions. The second motive is the precautionary motive, which is desire to hold money in the event of a need to make unplanned transactions. The third motive is the portfolio motive, which refers to the decision to hold a certain amount of money as part of an allocation of wealth among money and interest-bearing bonds, based on speculations about future changes in interest rates. The transactions and precautionary motives directly imply that the quantity of money demanded should depend directly on real income, while the portfolio motive indicates that the quantity of money demanded should vary inversely on the nominal interest rate.

Real money balances, or the real purchasing power of the nominal quantity of money, is equal to the nominal money stock divided by the GDP deflator, or $m = M/P$. Central banks influence the nominal money stock, but they cannot directly control the quantity of real money balances, because the price level is determined in markets for goods and services. Hence, the supply schedule for real money balances depends on both the nominal money stock and the price level. A fall in the nominal money stock reduces the supply of real money balances, while a rise in the nominal money stock raises the supply of real money balances. A rise in the price level reduces the supply of real money balances, whereas a fall in the price level raises the supply of real money balances.

According to Keynesian theory, the equilibrium nominal interest rate is the nominal interest rate at which the quantity of real money balances demanded is equal to the quantity of real money balances supplied. An increase in the nominal quantity of money supplied by the central bank, will, given an unchanged price level, induce a decline in the equilibrium nominal interest rate. This fall in the interest rate caused by an increase in the nominal quantity of money without a change in the price level is the liquidity effect of monetary policy. By way of contrast, an increase in the price level will, given an unchanged nominal quantity of money supplied by the central bank, induce a rise in the equilibrium nominal interest rate. This rise in the nominal interest rate caused by an increase in the price level without a change in the nominal money stock is called the real balance effect.

The *LM* schedule is a set of all combinations of real income levels and nominal rates of interest that maintain equilibrium in the market for real money balances, given a particular quantity of real money balances supplied by the central bank. A rise in real income raises the demand for real money balances, thereby inducing a rise in the equilibrium nominal interest rate. Thus, the *LM* schedule slopes upward. Its elasticity depends on the interest elasticity of the demand for real money balances. Around any given real income-interest rate combination, the *LM* schedule is relatively more elastic if the demand for real money balances is relatively more elastic. The position of the *LM* schedule depends on the quantity of real money balances supplied by the central bank. If the central bank were to increase the nominal money stock, then with an unchanged price level, the resulting rise in the supply of real money balances would shift the *LM* schedule downward and to the right. In contrast, a reduction in the money stock with an unchanged price level would shift the *LM* schedule upward and to the left. With the nominal money stock unchanged, however, an increase in the price level would reduce the supply of real money balances and shift the *LM* schedule upward and to the left. A decline in the price level with an unchanged nominal quantity of money would shift the *LM* schedule downward and to the right. The position of the *LM* schedule also can change in response to variations in the demand for real money balances not caused by a variation in real income. A decline in the demand for real money balances induced by a fall in real income would shift the *LM* schedule downward and to the right, while a rise in the demand for real money balances not caused by an increase in real income would, in contrast, shift the *LM* schedule upward and to the left.

The *IS* schedule is a set of real income-nominal interest rate combinations that maintain equality between real income and aggregate real desired expenditures. A reduction in the nominal interest rate will, if expected inflation is unchanged, result in a fall in the real interest rate that reduces desired investment spending and thereby cause a fall in equilibrium real income. Consequently, the *IS* schedule slopes downward. The elasticity of the *IS* schedule depends on the interest elasticity of desired investment.

Around a given real income-interest rate combination, if desired investment spending is relatively more interest elastic, then the derived IS schedule is relatively more elastic. The position of the *IS* schedule depends on autonomous net desired spending. At any given interest rate, reductions in autonomous saving, imports, or net taxes or increases in government expenditures or autonomous export spending would induce such an upward shift in the aggregated desired expenditures schedule, causing a rise in equilibrium real income equal to the increase in aggregate autonomous expenditures times the autonomous spending multiplier and a rightward shift of the *IS* schedule. Increases in autonomous saving, imports, or net taxes or reductions in government expenditures or autonomous export spending would induce such an downward shift in the aggregated desired expenditures schedule, inducing decline in equilibrium real income equal to the reduction in aggregate autonomous expenditures times the autonomous spending multiplier and a leftward shift of the *IS* schedule.

Because the *IS* schedule is a set of real income-nominal interest rate combinations that maintain equilibrium real income, and the *LM* schedule consists of real income-nominal interest rate combinations that maintain equilibrium in the market for real money balances, the single point at which the two schedules cross gives a single combination of real income and the nominal interest rate that achieves equilibrium real income while simultaneously achieving equilibrium in the market for real money balances. At any other real income-interest rate combination, there would be a tendency for real income and the nominal interest rate to move toward this point of *IS-LM* equilibrium.

Monetary policy actions that change the nominal money stock will, with an unchanged price level, alter the position of the *LM* schedule and change the location of an *IS-LM* equilibrium, thereby affecting the equilibrium nominal interest rate and the equilibrium level of real income. This forms the basis for the Keynesian monetary policy transmission mechanism. As shown in panel (a) of Figure 8, a reduction in the nominal money stock causes a liquidity effect that increases the equilibrium nominal interest rate. As depicted in panel (b), this causes a leftward shift of the *LM* schedule along the *IS* schedule, so that desired investment declines, thereby inducing a fall in equilibrium real income. The linkages in this mechanism are strengthened if the demand for real money balances is relatively interest-inelastic, so that the *LM* schedule is relatively inelastic, and if desired investment spending is relatively interest-elastic, so that the *IS* schedule is relatively elastic.

Figure 8: The Effects of a Reduction in the Money Stock in the *IS-LM* Framework

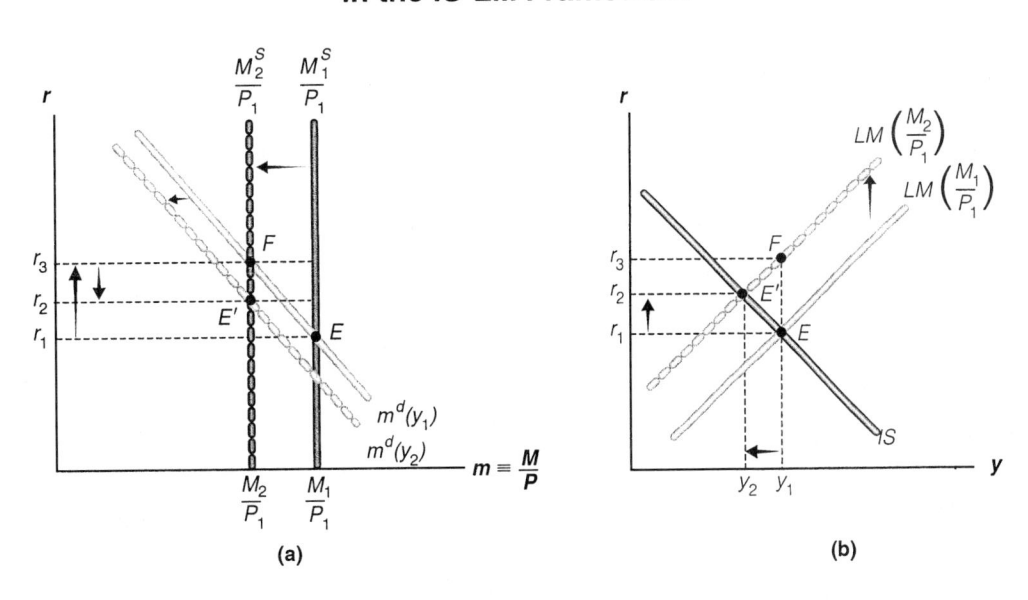

A rise in government expenditures causes the *IS* schedule to shift rightward by the amount of the spending increase times the autonomous expenditures multiplier, $1/(1-MPC)$. The resulting rise in real income causes an increase in the equilibrium nominal interest rate. If inflation expectations are unchanged, the rise in the nominal interest rate causes an increase in the real rate of interest, thereby inducing a decline in investment spending and, thus, aggregate desired expenditures. As a result, real income declines by the decline in investment spending times the autonomous expenditures multiplier, $1/(1-MPC)$. This reduction in investment spending is the crowding out effect of an increase in government spending that arises in the Keynesian *IS-LM* framework.

On net, there is not complete crowding out in the *IS-LM* model, so an increase in real government expenditures causes an increase in equilibrium real income. The amount of the net increase in equilibrium income depends on the size of the crowding-out effect, which in turn depends on the interest elasticities of desired investment and of the demand for real money balances. The crowding out effect is relatively larger if desired investment is relatively more interest-elastic, so that the *IS* schedule is relatively more elastic, and if the demand for real money balances is relatively more interest-inelastic, so that the *LM* schedule is relatively more inelastic.

A lump-sum tax cut has the same basic effects in the *IS-LM* model as those of a rise in government expenditures. The key difference is that the amount of a lump-sum tax reduction times the tax multiplier, $-MPC/(1-MPC)$ determines the amount of the shift of the *IS* schedule. Hence, a lump-sum tax reduction would cause both the equilibrium nominal interest rate and the equilibrium real income level to rise. The amount of the rise in real income would be lower than predicted by the Keynesian multiplier analysis owing to a crowding out effect resulting from a decline in investment spending owing to the increase in the interest rate.

Key Terms and Concepts

Interest-elastic demand for money
Interest-elastic desired investment
Interest-inelastic demand for money
Interest-inelastic desired investment
IS schedule
IS-LM equilibrium
Keynesian monetary policy transmission mechanism
Liquidity effect
LM schedule
Perpetuity
Portfolio motive
Precautionary motive
Real balance effect
Real money balances
Transactions motive

Multiple-Choice Questions

1. Recall that the Cambridge equation is $M^d = k \times Y$, where M^d denotes total desired money holdings, Y denotes total nominal income, and k represents the fraction of income that people wish to hold as money to use in planned exchanges for goods and services. Which of the following Keynesian motives for holding money could not be captured by the Cambridge equation?

    I. the precautionary motive
    II. the transactions motive
    III. the portfolio motive

    A) I only
    B) III only
    C) both I and II
    D) both II and III

2. The precautionary motive for holding money refers to the desire to hold money for use in

   A) previously planned transactions.
   B) previously unplanned transactions.
   C) speculating about bond price movements.
   D) speculating about interest rate movements.

3. The value from today's perspective of funds to be received at a future date is called the

   A) coupon return on the funds, if they are held in bonds.
   B) interest return on the funds, if they are held in bonds.
   C) discounted present value of the funds.
   D) determinate future value of the funds.

4. In the absence of risk and transactions costs entailed in holding and purchasing a bond with an infinite life, the price of the bond will, if the bond's annual coupon return is C and the market interest rate is r, be equal to

   A) $P_B = C/(1+r) + C/(1+r)^2 + C/(1+r)^3 + C/(1+r)^4 + \ldots$
   B) $P_B = C \times (1+r) + C \times (1+r)^2 + C \times (1+r)^3 + C \times (1+r)^4 + \ldots$
   C) $P_B = C/r + C/r^2 + C/r^3 + C/r^4 + \ldots$
   D) $P_B = C \times r + C \times r^2 + C \times r^3 + C \times r^4 + \ldots$

5. A liquidity effect that reduces the nominal interest rate refers to the effect of

   A) a fall in the price level that causes a decrease in the demand for real money balances.
   B) a rise in the price level that causes an increase in the demand for real money balances.
   C) a fall in the nominal quantity of money that causes a reduction in the supply of real money balances, holding the price level unchanged.
   D) a rise in the nominal quantity of money that causes an increase in the supply of real money balances, holding the price level unchanged.

6. The upward slope of the LM schedule reflects the fact that

   A) an increase in the price level causes a reduction in the demand for real money balances, thereby pushing up the equilibrium nominal interest rate.
   B) a reduction in the price level causes a reduction in the supply of real money balances, thereby pushing up the equilibrium nominal interest rate.
   C) an increase in real income causes an increase in the supply of real money balances, thereby pushing down the equilibrium nominal interest rate.
   D) a reduction in real income causes a reduction in the demand for real money balances, thereby pushing down the equilibrium nominal interest rate.

7. The downward slope of the *IS* schedule reflects the fact that

   A) an increase in the price level, will, with unchanged inflation expectations, cause a decline in desired real investment, thereby pushing up the equilibrium real interest rate.
   B) a reduction in the price level will, with unchanged inflation expectations, cause a rise in desired real investment, thereby pushing up the equilibrium real interest rate.
   C) an increase in the nominal interest rate will, with unchanged inflation expectations, cause a decline in desired real investment, thereby pushing down equilibrium real income.
   D) a reduction in the nominal interest rate will, with unchanged inflation expectations, cause a decline in desired real investment, thereby pushing down equilibrium real income.

8. Which of the following could result in a leftward shift of the *IS* schedule?

   I. a reduction in net taxes
   II. a reduction in real export spending
   III. a reduction in real government spending

   A) both I and II only
   B) both I and III only
   C) both II and III only
   D) I, II, and III

9. Which of the following could result in a rightward shift of the *IS* schedule?

   I. a reduction in autonomous saving
   II. a reduction in autonomous imports
   III. a reduction in real government spending

   A) both I and II only
   B) both I and III only
   C) both II and III only
   D) I, II, and III

10. Suppose that the demand for real money balances is highly interest-elastic, but desired investment is highly interest-inelastic. In this situation, we may conclude from the *IS-LM* model that

   I.   the *LM* schedule is highly elastic.
   II. the *IS* schedule is highly inelastic.
   III. an increase in the quantity of money causes the nominal interest rate to rise.

   A) both I and II only
   B) both I and III only
   C) both II and III only
   D) I, II, and III

11. According to the Keynesian transmission mechanism for monetary policy, a reduction in the nominal money stock

   A) pushes up the price level, thereby reducing equilibrium real income.
   B) pushes the price level down, thereby reducing the equilibrium nominal interest rate.
   C) pushes up the equilibrium nominal interest rate, thereby reducing desired investment spending and equilibrium real income.
   D) pushes up equilibrium real income, thereby raising desired investment spending and the equilibrium nominal interest rate.

12. Which of the following would tend to strengthen the linkages in the Keynesian monetary policy transmission mechanism?

   I.   highly interest-elastic *IS* schedule
   II. highly interest-inelastic money demand
   III. highly interest-inelastic desired investment

   A) I only
   B) III only
   C) both I and II
   D) both II and III

13. At a point below the *LM* schedule and to the right of the *IS* schedule,

    I. Equilibrium real income is attained, but the quantity of real money balances demanded exceeds the quantity of real money balances supplied.
    II. The market for real money balances is in equilibrium, but businesses accumulate undesired inventories of finished goods.
    III. The nominal interest rate will begin to rise, and real income will begin to decline.

    A) I only
    B) III only
    C) both I and II
    D) both II and III

14. At the single point at which the *IS* and *LM* schedules cross,

    I. The market for real money balances is in equilibrium.
    II. Real income is equal to aggregate desired expenditures.
    III. Leakages from the aggregate spending flow equal reinjections into that flow.

    A) both I and II only
    B) both I and III only
    C) both II and III only
    D) I, II, and III

15. A key reason that an increase in real government expenditures can crowd out private spending is that a rise in government spending can induce

    A) a reduction in the demand for real money balances.
    B) a reduction in equilibrium real income.
    C) a rise in real desired investment.
    D) a rise in the interest rate.

16. An increase in real government expenditures causes the IS schedule to shift rightward

    A) by the amount of the spending increase times the autonomous expenditures multiplier, ultimately resulting in a somewhat smaller rise in equilibrium real income.
    B) along the LM schedule, which thereby inducing an increase in the demand for real money balances that in turn causes the LM schedule to shift upward and to the right.
    C) along the LM schedule, which thereby always raises equilibrium real income by the amount of the spending increase times the autonomous expenditures multiplier.
    D) by exactly the amount of the increase in government spending, eventually resulting in an increase in equilibrium real income by the amount of the spending increase.

17. In the Keynesian IS-LM framework, the crowding-out effect becomes larger if

    I. the demand for real money balances becomes relatively more interest-inelastic.
    II. desired investment spending becomes relatively more interest-inelastic.
    III. the autonomous expenditures multiplier becomes smaller.

    A) I only
    B) II only
    C) both I and III
    D) both II and III

18. If there is a decline in the demand for money caused by the increased use of credit cards at the same time that the government enacts a tax reduction, then if all other factors including the price level are unchanged, the IS-LM model predicts that the results would be

    A) a rise in equilibrium real income but an indeterminate effect on the equilibrium nominal interest rate.
    B) a fall in equilibrium real income but an indeterminate effect on the equilibrium nominal interest rate.
    C) a rise in the equilibrium nominal interest rate but an indeterminate effect on equilibrium real income.
    D) a fall in the equilibrium nominal interest rate but an indeterminate effect on equilibrium real income.

19. Suppose that a nation's government reduces its spending at the same time that the nation's central bank reduces the nominal quantity of money. Then, holding other factors such as the price level unchanged, the *IS-LM* model indicates that the results would be

    A) a rise in equilibrium real income but an indeterminate effect on the equilibrium nominal interest rate.
    B) a fall in equilibrium real income but an indeterminate effect on the equilibrium nominal interest rate.
    C) a rise in the equilibrium nominal interest rate but an indeterminate effect on equilibrium real income.
    D) a fall in the equilibrium nominal interest rate but an indeterminate effect on equilibrium real income.

20. Suppose that a nation's government raises net taxes at the same time that the nation's central bank increases the nominal quantity of money. Then, holding other factors such as the price level unchanged, the *IS-LM* model indicates that the results would be

    A) a rise in equilibrium real income but an indeterminate effect on the equilibrium nominal interest rate.
    B) a fall in equilibrium real income but an indeterminate effect on the equilibrium nominal interest rate.
    C) a rise in the equilibrium nominal interest rate but an indeterminate effect on equilibrium real income.
    D) a fall in the equilibrium nominal interest rate but an indeterminate effect on equilibrium real income.

Short-Answer Questions

1. What kind of bond never matures?

2. What is the *LM* schedule?

3. What is the interest elasticity of the demand for real money balances?

4. What is the *IS* schedule?

5. What is the interest elasticity of desired investment?

6. What is the real balance effect on the nominal interest rate?

7. What is the liquidity effect on the nominal interest rate?

8. What is the Keynesian monetary transmission mechanism?

9. Under what conditions does no crowding out take place in the Keynesian model?

10. Under what conditions does complete crowding out take place in the Keynesian model?

Chapter 9: The Open Economy — Exchange Rates and the Balance of Payments

Chapter Summary

The *BP* schedule is a set of combinations of real income and the nominal interest rate that achieve a particular value, such as zero, for the private payments balance. Hence, an *IS-LM* equilibrium at a point along the *BP* schedule achieves private payments balance. At an *IS-LM* equilibrium above and to the left of the *BP* schedule, the nominal interest rate is sufficiently high to attract inflows of financial assets from other nations, and real income is sufficiently low to depress imports, resulting in a private payments surplus. At an *IS-LM* equilibrium below and to the right of the *BP* schedule, the nominal interest rate is sufficiently low to spur outflows of financial assets to other nations, and real income is sufficiently high to spur imports, resulting in a private payments deficit. The *IS-LM-BP* framework illustrates the potential tradeoff that a central bank may face in efforts to achieve domestic real income, or internal balance, objectives at the same time that it pursues objectives for the private payments balance, or external balance.

A nation with high capital mobility is one that permits considerable flows of financial assets across its borders, whereas a country with low capital mobility often has legal impediments called capital controls that restrict the ability of the country's residents to hold and exchange assets denominated in the currencies of other nations. In a country with low capital mobility, the *BP* schedule is relatively steep, because if real income were to rise and cause an increase in imports and a current account deficit to occur, then a relatively large interest-rate increase would be needed to induce foreigners to undertake the expense of overcoming barriers to flows of financial assets that would be necessary to improve the nation's capital account balance sufficiently to reattain private payments balance. In contrast, with high capital mobility the *BP* schedule is relatively shallow.

When a nation experiences both a government budget deficit and a private payments deficit, the appropriate fiscal policy actions to try to reduce both deficits under a fixed exchange rate depend on the degree of capital mobility. A private payments deficit arises at an *IS-LM* equilibrium point to the right of the *BP* schedule, and so attaining private payment balance would, with low capital mobility, require a leftward shift of the *IS* schedule to reduce real income and stem imports. Raising taxes, reducing government expenditures, or a combination of both types of fiscal policy actions would reduce both deficits simultaneously. If capital mobility is very high, however, a rightward shift of the *IS* schedule would be needed to raise the nominal interest rate and induce capital inflows. Hence, the government would need to reduce taxes or increase its spending, which would, if other factors are unchanged, widen the government's budget deficit.

If the exchange rate floats, then the position of the *BP* schedule changes as the exchange rate adjusts in the face of private payments deficits or surpluses. If there is a private payments deficit, domestic residents make more payments to foreign residents than foreign residents make to domestic residents. On net, this raises the demand for foreign currencies relative to the domestic currency, which causes the domestic currency to depreciate. This induces domestic residents to reduce their imports at any given level of real income and interest rate, causing the BP schedule to shift to the right until the private payments deficit disappears. Irrespective of the degree of capital mobility, therefore, a government facing a both a budget deficit and a private payments deficit could reduce its spending or raise taxes to reduce the government budget deficit and allow exchange-rate adjustments to reduce the private payments deficit.

The central bank of a nation with fixed exchange rates must decide whether or not to conduct sterilized monetary policies, in which the central bank prevents changes in foreign exchange reserves from affecting its nation's money stock. A private payments deficit tends to cause a nation's currency to depreciate, requiring the central bank to sell foreign exchange reserves to maintain a fixed exchange rate. In the absence of monetary policy sterilization, the result is a decline in the nation's money stock. According to the monetary approach to the balance of payments, this implies that an expansionary, unsterilized increase in the nominal money stock that initially raises real income, reduces the nominal interest rate, and induces a private payments deficit ultimately requires an offsetting decline in the nominal money stock, so that real income and the interest rate on net remain unaffected.

With fixed exchange rates, the effects on equilibrium real income and the equilibrium interest rate of a bond-financed rise in government spending depend on the degree of capital mobility. If capital mobility is low, then the result would be a private payments deficit, because the rise in the interest rate would induce insufficient capital inflows to compensate for the rise in the trade deficit resulting from the resulting increases in real income and imports. Under the monetary approach to the balance of payments, the central bank would need to respond to downward pressure on the nation's currency value by selling foreign exchange reserves. With unsterilized monetary policy, the result would be a decline in the quantity of money that would tend to reduce the increase in equilibrium real income. In contrast, if capital mobility is high, there would be a private payments surplus, because significant capital inflows resulting from the higher equilibrium interest rate would cause a capital account surplus would more than counterbalance the trade deficit resulting from higher income and imports. According to the monetary approach to the balance of payments, the central bank would need to respond to upward pressure on the nation's currency value by buying foreign exchange reserves. With unsterilized monetary policy, the result would be a rise in the quantity of money that would tend to reinforce the increase in equilibrium real income.

With floating exchange rates, with either high or low capital mobility a reduction of the money stock shifts the *LM* schedule leftward, thereby resulting in a movement from point *A* to point *B* in Figure9. The decline in equilibrium real income induces a decline in imports and a rise in the nominal interest rate that induces capital inflows. Both occurrences lead to a private payments surplus at point *B*, and the nation's currency appreciates. The domestic currency appreciation causes the BP schedule to shift upward and to the left, from BP_1 to BP_2, and it stimulates a reduction in exports, so the *IS* schedule shifts leftward, from IS_1 to IS_2. Hence, there is a reattainment of private payments balance at point *C*.

Figure 9: The Effects of a Decrease in the Money Stock with Floating Exchange Rates

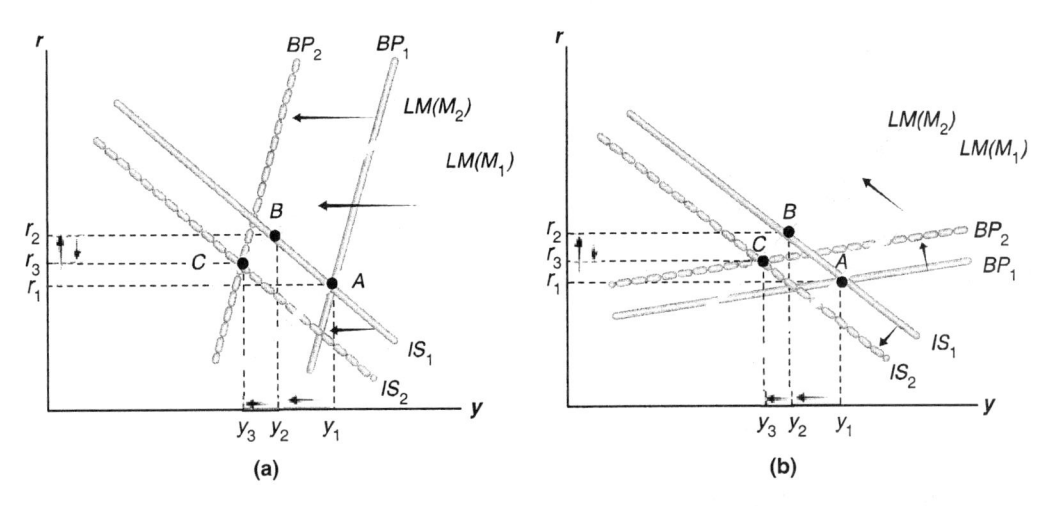

The effects of fiscal policy actions under floating exchange rates depend on the degree of capital mobility. If capital mobility is low, then the result of a bond-financed increase in government expenditures would be a private payments deficit that would lead to a currency depreciation and a consequent rise in exports that would push the value of the private payments balance back toward zero. By way of contrast, if capital mobility is high, there would be a private payments surplus that would lead to a currency appreciation and a resulting decline in exports that would push the value of the private payments balance back toward zero.

Key Terms and Concepts

BP schedule
Capital controls
Capital mobility
External balance
Internal balance
Monetary approach to the balance of payments
Sterilization

Multiple-Choice Questions

1. External balance refers to

   A) preventing depreciation in a nation's currency value.
   B) attaining a surplus in the overall balance of payments.
   C) attaining an overall balance of payments equal to zero.
   D) achieving a goal value for the private payments balance.

2. Internal balance refers to

   A) attainment of an objective for a domestic macroeconomic variable such as real income.
   B) achieving a level of domestic real income that keeps the exchange rate unchanged.
   C) preventing a domestic government budget deficit or surplus from affecting the exchange rate.
   D) preventing a domestic government budget deficit of surplus from affecting the private payments balance.

3. Along the *BP* schedule,

   A) the quantity of real money balances demanded equals the quantity of real money balances supplied.
   B) real income equals aggregate desired expenditures.
   C) there is a private payments balance equal to zero.
   D) the exchange rate is fixed.

4. At the real income level corresponding to a point to the right of a nation's *BP* schedule,

   A) the nominal interest rate is sufficiently high that real desired investment declines, causing equilibrium real income to fall.
   B) the nominal interest rate is sufficiently low that capital flows out of the nation, thereby contributing to a private payments deficit.
   C) the nominal interest rate is sufficiently low that real desired investment increases, causing equilibrium real income to rise.
   D) the nominal interest rate is sufficiently high that capital flows into the nation, thereby contributing to a private payments surplus.

The Open Economy — Exchange Rates and the Balance of Payments 91

5. At the interest rate corresponding to a point to the left of a nation's *BP* schedule,

   A) real income is sufficiently high that the demand for money increases, causing the nominal interest rate to rise.
   B) real income is sufficiently low that the demand for money declines, causing the nominal interest rate to decline.
   C) real income is sufficiently high that imports rise, thereby contributing to a private payments deficit.
   D) real income is sufficiently low that imports fall, thereby contributing to a private payments surplus.

6. Which of the following is true at a point of *IS-LM* equilibrium along a nation's *BP* schedule?

   I. The quantity of real money balances demanded equals the quantity of real money balances supplied.
   II. Real income is equal to aggregate real desired expenditures at the current nominal interest rate.
   III. The overall balance of payments is equal to zero, and there is a private payments surplus

   A) both I and II only
   B) both I and III only
   C) both II and III only
   D) I, II, and III

7. Which of the following is true at an *IS-LM* equilibrium above the *BP* schedule?

   I. Leakages from the aggregate spending flow equal reinjections into that flow.
   II. The overall balance of payments is equal to zero, and there is a private payments surplus.
   III. The quantity of real money balances demanded exceeds the quantity of real money balances supplied.

   A) both I and II only
   B) both I and III only
   C) both II and III only
   D) I, II, and III

8. Suppose that the exchange rate is fixed and capital mobility is very low. Which one of the following statements is correct?

    A) The nation's *BP* schedule is very shallow.
    B) The nation's *BP* schedule will shift in response to a private payments deficit or surplus.
    C) If the government faces both a budget deficit and a private payments deficit, a reduction in government spending will tend to reduce both deficits.
    D) If the government faces both a budget deficit and a private payments deficit, a reduction in government spending will reduce the private payments deficit but not the government's budget deficit.

9. Suppose that the exchange rate is fixed and capital mobility is very high. Which one of the following statements is correct?

    A) The nation's *BP* schedule is very shallow.
    B) The nation's *BP* schedule will shift in response to a private payments deficit or surplus.
    C) If the government faces both a budget deficit and a private payments deficit, a reduction in government spending will tend to reduce both deficits.
    D) If the government faces both a budget deficit and a private payments deficit, a reduction in government spending will reduce the private payments deficit but not the government's budget deficit.

10. Which of the following could contribute to making the *BP* schedule more steeply sloped?

    I.   highly interest elastic money demand
    II. the imposition of capital controls
    III. highly mobile financial assets

    A) I only
    B) II only
    C) both I and III
    D) both II and III

11. If a nation's exchange rate floats, then which of the following statements is correct?

    A) If there is a private payments deficit, then the nation's currency tends to appreciate, causing a rightward shift of the *BP* schedule.
    B) If there is a private payments deficit, then the nation's currency tends to depreciate, causing a rightward shift of the *BP* schedule.
    C) If there is a private payments deficit, then the nation's currency tends to appreciate, causing a leftward shift of the *BP* schedule.
    D) If there is a private payments deficit, then the nation's currency tends to depreciate, causing a leftward shift of the *BP* schedule.

12. Suppose that a nation's exchange rate floats. Then if a government faces both a budget deficit and a private payments deficit and does not wish to change taxes, eliminating the two deficits will entail _____ government spending and permitting the nation's currency to _____.

    A) reducing; appreciate.
    B) reducing; depreciate.
    C) raising; appreciate.
    D) raising; depreciate.

13. According to the monetary approach to the balance of payments, when the central bank seeks to maintain a fixed exchange rate,

    A) a private payments deficit automatically induces a depreciation that leads to reattainment of private payments balance.
    B) a private payments deficit automatically induces a fall in the money stock that leads to reattainment of private payments balance.
    C) a key component of the nominal quantity of money is the private payments balance, which thereby adjusts automatically to monetary policy actions.
    D) a key component of the private payments balance is the nominal quantity of money, which automatically adjusts to eliminate private payments deficits.

14. Suppose that a nation's central bank strives to keep the exchange rate fixed, and suppose that initially the nation has attained private payments balance. In an effort to induce a short-run contraction in real income, the central bank reduces the nation's money stock. Which of the following provides a possible explanation of the adjustments that might follow this action?

    A) The fall in real income would induce a decline in imports and a private payments surplus, so unsterilized central bank purchases of foreign exchange reserves to keep the exchange rate unchanged would cause the money stock to rise toward its original level.
    B) The fall in real income would induce a decline in imports and a private payments surplus, so sterilized central bank purchases of foreign exchange reserves to keep the exchange rate unchanged would cause the money stock to rise toward its original level.
    C) The resulting decline in the nominal interest rate would cause a private payments surplus to arise as financial assets flowed into the nation, so the central bank would have to reduce the nominal money stock further to reattain private payments balance.
    D) The resulting decline in the nominal interest rate would cause a private payments surplus to arise as financial assets flowed into the nation, so the central bank would have to conduct sterilized foreign exchange interventions to induce a rise in the money stock and reattain private payments balance.

15. Consider a nation with a fixed exchange rate and relatively low capital mobility. Which of the following explains how fiscal policy actions can place pressure on the nation's central bank to devalue the nation's currency?

   A) Persistent increases in government spending induce private payments deficits that require the central bank to sell foreign exchange reserves, and the ultimate depletion of these reserves can necessitate a devaluation.
   B) Persistent increases in government spending induce private payments surpluses that require the central bank to buy foreign exchange reserves, and excessive accumulation of reserves can necessitate a devaluation.
   C) Persistent reductions in government spending induce private payments deficits that require the central bank to sell foreign exchange reserves, and the ultimate depletion of these reserves can necessitate a devaluation.
   D) Persistent reductions in government spending induce private payments surpluses that require the central bank to buy foreign exchange reserves, and excessive accumulation of reserves can necessitate a devaluation.

16. If a central bank that fixes exchange rates sterilizes its foreign exchange market interventions, then

   A) purchases of foreign-currency-denominated assets increase the money stock.
   B) purchases of foreign-currency-denominated assets reduce the money stock.
   C) sales of foreign-currency-denominated assets have no effect on the money stock.
   D) sales of foreign-currency-denominated assets cause the money stock to increase.

17. In a nation with very high capital mobility, the immediate effect of an expansionary monetary policy action is a private payments

   A) deficit, primarily because of the resulting fall in imports.
   B) surplus, primarily because of the resulting increase in imports.
   C) deficit, primarily because of the resulting increase in capital outflows.
   D) surplus, primarily because of the resulting increase in capital inflows.

18. If the exchange rate floats and capital mobility is very low, then

    I. the BP schedule is very steeply sloped.
    II. an expansionary monetary policy action is likely to induce a private payments surplus that would result in a currency appreciation.
    III. a contractionary fiscal policy action is likely to induce a private payments surplus that would result in a currency appreciation.

    A) II only
    B) III only
    C) both I and II
    D) both I and III

19. If the exchange rate floats and capital mobility is very high, then

    I. the BP schedule is very shallowly sloped.
    II. a contractionary fiscal policy action is likely to induce a private payments deficit that would result in a currency depreciation.
    III. an expansionary monetary policy action is likely to induce a private payments deficit that would result in a currency appreciation.

    A) I only
    B) III only
    C) both I and II
    D) both II and III

20. If the exchange rate floats and capital mobility is very high, then an increase in real government spending induces which of the following chains of events?

    A) a private payments deficit, which results in a currency depreciation, an increase in exports, and a movement back toward private payments balance.
    B) a private payments deficit, which results in a currency appreciation, a reduction in exports, and a movement back toward private payments balance.
    C) a private payments surplus, which results in a currency depreciation, an increase in exports, and a movement back toward private payments balance.
    D) a private payments surplus, which results in a currency appreciation, a reduction in exports, and a movement back toward private payments balance.

Short-Answer Questions

1. What is internal balance?

2. What is external balance?

3. What is the *BP* schedule?

4. What is capital mobility?

5. What are capital controls?

6. What key factor determines the slope of the *BP* schedule?

7. What key factor determines the position of the *BP* schedule?

8. What is monetary policy sterilization?

9. What is the key implication of the monetary approach to the balance of payments for monetary policy when there is a fixed change rate?

10. What is the key implication of the monetary approach to the balance of payments for fiscal policy when there is a fixed exchange rate and relatively high capital mobility?

Chapter 10: Is There a Tradeoff Between Unemployment and Inflation? — The Keynesian and Monetarist Views on Price and Output Determination

Chapter Summary

A rise in the price level reduces the supply of real money balances, thereby causing the nominal interest rate to rise at any given level of real income. This real balance effect causes the *LM* schedule to shift upward and to the left, thereby reducing equilibrium real income. Hence, the Keynesian *IS-LM* model implies a downward-sloping relationship between the price level and real income, which is the Keynesian aggregate demand schedule. This schedule consists of real income-price level combinations that maintain *IS-LM* equilibrium, given the nominal quantity of money in circulation and autonomous net aggregate expenditures. Consequently, changes in the nominal money stock or in autonomous expenditures, such as government spending and taxation and autonomous consumption, investment, and net exports, induce shifts in the aggregate demand schedule.

The Keynesian theory of aggregate supply departs from the classical theory by considering the possibilities that nominal wages might be inflexible or that workers might have imperfect information about the price level. If wages are inflexible, perhaps because of legal impediments to wage adjustments or explicit or implicit contracts between workers and firms, then workers supply whatever amount of labor that firms demand at the fixed nominal wage. A price increase that raises the value of the marginal product of labor thereby increases labor demand and employment, causing real output to rise. Consequently, there is an upward-sloping aggregate supply schedule if the nominal wage is fixed, and this schedule shifts upward and to the left if nominal wages rise.

If workers have incomplete information about the overall price level, they must base their decisions about how much labor to supply on their price expectations. As a result, the position of the labor supply schedule depends on the expected price level. A rise in the actual price level causes an increase the value of the marginal product of labor increases at firms, yielding a rise in labor demand, an upward movement along the labor supply schedule, and an increase in the equilibrium nominal wage. If workers are unaware that the actual price level has risen, then they interpret the nominal wage increase as a rise in the real wage, and they increase the amount of labor supplied to firms. As a result, employment and output increase, and the aggregate supply schedule slopes upward. An increase in the expected price level would shift the aggregate supply schedule upward and to the left.

In the Keynesian model, the equilibrium price level and real output level arise at the point at which the aggregate demand schedule crosses the upward-sloping aggregate supply schedule, such as the initial equilibrium point E depicted in panel (a) of Figure 10. Because this point is on the aggregate demand schedule, real income is equal to aggregate desired expenditures, and the quantity of real money balances demanded is equal to the real value of the quantity of money balances supplied. In addition, because this point is also on the aggregate supply schedule, workers and firms are willing and able to produce the equilibrium level of real output. Fiscal and monetary policy actions influence equilibrium real output and prices in the traditional Keynesian model by inducing shifts in the aggregate demand schedule. Such policy actions can affect both the equilibrium price level and the equilibrium level of output because of the upward slope of the Keynesian aggregate supply schedule. The figure, for instance, shows the effect of a reduction in the nominal money stock, which shifts the *LM* schedule leftward in panel (a), thereby inducing a leftward shift in the aggregate demand schedule in panel (b). The result is a decline in the equilibrium price level that shifts the *LM* schedule back to the right somewhat. On net, equilibrium real output declines.

Figure 10: The Price-Level and Real-Output Effects of a Reduction in the Money Stock in the Keynesian Model

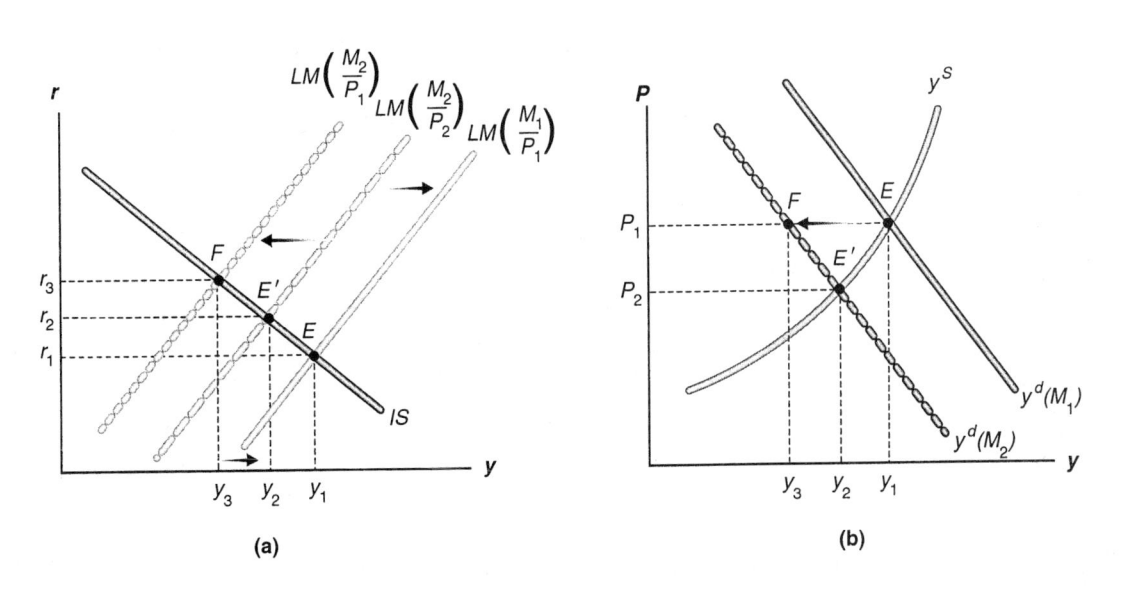

A Phillips curve is a plot of the relationship between unemployment and inflation rates. The Keynesian theory of aggregate supply implies that the Phillips curve should slope downward, so that there is an inverse relationship between the unemployment rate and the inflation rate, as the United States experienced during the 1960s.

Consequently, the traditional Keynesian theory of price level-real output determination indicates that policymakers could, in principle, choose an inflation rate-unemployment rate combination based on social preferences concerning unemployment and inflation.

Proponents of monetarism, who traditionally emphasized money as the primary determinant of aggregate demand, challenged the Keynesian view that the Phillips curve was a stable, downward-sloping relationship. They argued that a inverse relationship between unemployment rates and inflation rates can apply only to a short-run interval in which information is imperfect and expected inflation rates are not necessarily equal to actual inflation rates. In the long run, the monetarists argued, inflation expectations adjust to equality with actual inflation, so that the aggregate supply schedule is vertical, as in the classical model. As a result, the economy achieves long-run, natural levels of output and employment and operates at a natural rate of unemployment that does not vary with inflation. At this natural unemployment rate, therefore, the long-run Phillips curve is vertical.

The monetarist theory of the short-run and long-run Phillips curves is the foundation for the political-business-cycle theory. This theory indicates that politically motivated efforts to reduce unemployment can lead to higher inflation and inflation expectations. In the short run, this causes a movement along a short-run Phillips curve and results in lower unemployment. In the long run, as inflation expectations rise, the short-run Phillips curve shifts up along the vertical, long-run Phillips curve, and the unemployment rate ultimately rises back to the natural unemployment rate. During an interval of long-run adjustment with both rising inflation and rising unemployment, the economy experiences stagflation.

Key Terms and Concepts

Explicit contracts
Implicit contracts
Long run
Monetarists
Natural rate of unemployment
Phillips curve
Short run
Stagflation

Multiple-Choice Questions

1. The downward slope of the Keynesian aggregate demand schedule results from

    A) the policy transmission effect.
    B) the crowding-out effect.
    C) the real balance effect.
    D) the liquidity effect.

2. Which of the following is true at any given point along the Keynesian aggregate demand schedule?

    I. The market for real money balances is in equilibrium.
    II. Real income equals aggregate desired expenditures.
    III. The market for labor is in equilibrium.

    A) I only
    B) III only
    C) both I and II
    D) both II and III

3. Which of the following could help to explain an upward-sloping aggregate supply schedule?

    I. equiproportionate movements of nominal wages with price changes
    II. imperfect information about the aggregate price level
    III. inflexibility of nominal wages owing to labor contracts

    A) I only
    B) III only
    C) both I and II
    D) both II and III

4. The constitution of the Federal Republic of Germany calls for the establishment of a base nominal wage rate via the coordination of wage agreements among large unions and corporations. If the current German price level is high and current German real GDP is low, relative to socially desired levels, then a new set of labor agreements that specifies higher nominal wages would shift the

A) aggregate supply schedule leftward, thereby inducing a further decline in real GDP and a further increase in the price level.
B) aggregate demand schedule leftward, thereby inducing a further decline in real GDP while pushing the price level down toward the desired level.
C) aggregate demand schedule rightward, thereby inducing a rise in real GDP while pushing the price level even further above the desired level.
D) aggregate supply schedule rightward, thereby inducing a rise in real GDP and a reduction in the German price level that push both toward desired levels.

5. Consider a nation in which nominal wages are flexible but information about the aggregate price level is imperfect. If people were to suddenly anticipate a rise in the price level, in spite of recent stability of the equilibrium price level, then the result would be

A) a reduction in the real wage that induces a rise in the equilibrium amount of labor employed by firms.
B) a rise in the demand for labor by firms that results in an increase in the equilibrium real wage and an rise in equilibrium employment.
C) a leftward movement along the aggregate supply schedule and corresponding reductions in equilibrium real output and the equilibrium price level.
D) a leftward shift of the aggregate supply schedule and a corresponding reduction in equilibrium real output and increase in the equilibrium price level.

6. In the Keynesian model, which of the following must be true at a point of equilibrium in the market for real output?

  I. The Phillips curve is vertical at the unemployment rate that arises at the equilibrium output level.
  II. At the equilibrium price level and level of real output, there is a corresponding IS-LM equilibrium.
  III. At the equilibrium price level, workers and firms are willing and able to produce the corresponding level of output.

A) I only
B) III only
C) both I and II
D) both II and III

7. Suppose that a nation's central bank reduces the nominal money stock at the same time that most of the nation's workers agree to accept a nominal wage cut. As a result, in the Keynesian market for real output the equilibrium price level

   A) will rise, but equilibrium real output may rise or fall.
   B) will decline, but equilibrium real output may rise or fall.
   C) may rise or fall, but equilibrium real output will decline.
   D) may rise or fall, but equilibrium real output will increase.

8. Suppose that a nation's government enacts a lump-sum tax cut at the same time that the bulk of a nation's residents anticipate an increase in the price level. As a result, in the Keynesian market for real output the equilibrium price level

   A) will rise, but equilibrium real output may rise or fall.
   B) will decline, but equilibrium real output may rise or fall.
   C) may rise or fall, but equilibrium real output will decline.
   D) may rise or fall, but equilibrium real output will increase.

9. Suppose that a sharp decline in overall energy prices occurs at the same time that a nation's government increases its real spending. As a result, in the Keynesian market for real output the equilibrium price level

   A) will rise, but equilibrium real output may rise or fall.
   B) will decline, but equilibrium real output may rise or fall.
   C) may rise or fall, but equilibrium real output will decline.
   D) may rise or fall, but equilibrium real output will increase.

10. Which of the following is true of the Keynesian model?

    I. Both monetary and fiscal policy actions affect aggregate demand.
    II. The short-run aggregate supply schedule slopes upward.
    III. The short-run Phillips curve slopes upward.

    A) I only
    B) III only
    C) both I and II
    D) both II and III

11. Along the short-run Phillips curve,

    A) there is a direct relationship between the actual inflation rate and the unemployment rate.
    B) there is an inverse relationship between the actual inflation rate and the unemployment rate.
    C) there is a direct relationship between the expected inflation rate and the unemployment rate.
    D) there is an inverse relationship between the expected inflation rate and the unemployment rate.

12. Which of the following could induce a rightward shift of the short-run Phillips curve?

    I. an increase in inflation expectations
    II. an overall rise in contracted nominal wages
    III. a rightward shift of the aggregate supply schedule

    A) both I and II only
    B) both I and III only
    C) both II and III only
    D) I, II, and III

13. Along the long-run Phillips curve,

    A) the expected inflation rate is equal to the actual inflation rate.
    B) the expected unemployment rate is equal to the actual unemployment rate.
    C) there is a direct relationship between the actual inflation rate and the unemployment rate.
    D) there is an inverse relationship between the actual inflation rate and the unemployment rate.

14. At the point at which a short-run Phillips curve crosses the long-run Phillips curve,

    I. the actual unemployment rate equals the natural unemployment rate
    II. both the short-run and long-run Phillips curves are vertical.
    III. the expected inflation rate equals the actual inflation rate.

    A) both I and II only
    B) both I and III only
    C) both II and III only
    D) I, II, and III

15. If the short-run aggregate supply schedule is vertical, then

    A) the short-run Phillips curve is vertical.
    B) the short-run Phillips curve is horizontal.
    C) an increase in government spending is noninflationary.
    D) an increase in the nominal money stock is noninflationary.

16. According to the monetarist theory, an increase in the growth of the nominal quantity of money causes

    A) a short-run increase in the unemployment rate that is ultimately followed by a decline in the unemployment rate to its natural level.
    B) a short-run decrease in the unemployment rate that is ultimately followed by an increase in the unemployment rate to its natural level.
    C) a short-run increase in the inflation rate that is ultimately offset by a long-run reduction in the inflation rate.
    D) a short-run reduction in the inflation rate that is ultimately offset by a long-run increase in the inflation rate.

17. According to the monetarist theory, a reduction in the growth of the nominal quantity of money causes

    A) a short-run decrease in the unemployment rate that is ultimately reinforced by a further decline in the unemployment rate to its natural level.
    B) a short-run increase in the unemployment rate that is ultimately reinforced by a further rise in the unemployment rate to its natural level.
    C) a short-run reduction in the inflation rate that is ultimately reinforced by a further long-run reduction in the inflation rate.
    D) a short-run increase in the inflation rate that is ultimately reinforced by a further long-run rise in the inflation rate.

18. Of the following decades, the one during which the Keynesian theory of the Phillips curve received the clearest support from U.S. inflation and unemployment experience was the

    A) 1990s.
    B) 1980s.
    C) 1970s.
    D) 1960s.

19. According to the political-business-cycle model, in the long run politically motivated attempts to reduce the unemployment rate below its natural rate result in

   I. reduced inflation expectations.
   II. a higher actual inflation rate.
   III. a lower unemployment rate.

   A) I only
   B) II only
   C) both I and III
   D) both II and III

20. According to the political-business-cycle model, in the long run politically motivated attempts to reduce the inflation rate result in

   I. reduced inflation expectations.
   II. a higher unemployment rate.
   III. a lower actual inflation rate.

   A) I only
   B) II only
   C) both I and III
   D) both II and III

Short-Answer Questions

1. What is true at any point along a Keynesian aggregate demand schedule?

2. What is a tacit agreement between workers and firms that theoretically can produce nominal wage inflexibility?

3. If the nominal wage is fixed via a labor contract, what determines the level of employment?

4. What factors could account for an upward-sloping aggregate supply schedule?

5. Under what circumstance is money nonneutral in its real output effects?

6. According to the Monetarist theory, what constitutes the "short run"?

7. According to the Monetarist theory, what constitutes the "long run"?

8. What is the term for the unemployment rate that is determined by the position of the long-run Phillips curve?

9. What is true of the expected inflation rate at any point along a short-run Phillips curve?

10. What is true of the expected inflation rate at any point along a long-run Phillips curve?

Chapter 11: The Pursuit of Self-Interest — Rational Expectations, New Classical Macroeconomics, and Efficient Markets

Chapter Summary

Modern macroeconomic theories explicitly include depictions of expectations formation processes. There are two types of expectations formation processes: adaptive expectations and rational expectations. An adaptive expectation process entails using only past information as a basis for a forecast. A key drawback with this approach to modeling expectations is that adaptive expectations can be persistently incorrect, and so the people whose behavior the model attempts to describe would behave inconsistently. Another problem is that it is not possible to determine what adaptive expectations process gives the "best" forecast.

According to the rational expectations hypothesis, a person makes the best possible forecast using all available past and current information and drawing on an understanding of what factors affect the macroeconomic variable. In contrast to a purely backward-looking adaptive forecast, a rational forecast also looks forward while also taking into account past information. Under this expectation formation process, if a person can improve upon an adaptive forecast, she or he will do so. A rationally formed expectation need not be correct, but a rational-expectation process does not yield persistently incorrect forecasts. To include the hypothesis of rational expectations in their theories, macroeconomists typically adopt representative agent assumption, under which a macroeconomic model presumes that each person in the economy has the same information and has an identical view of how the economy works. They also assume that everyone in the economy understands how the economy functions.

The new classical economists were the first to adopt the rational expectations hypothesis. As in the classical theory, the basis new classical model assumes that people are motivated by self-interest, that pure competition prevails and that wages and prices are completely flexible. In contrast to the classical theory, however, new classical economists assume that no one has complete information. Nevertheless, they assume that all individuals form expectations of the price level and inflation rate rationally, using all available past and current information and their understanding of how the economy functions.

This means that people must track current policies and try to forecast future policies, because they know that policy actions will influence the price level. As a result, workers' price-level expectation, P^e, depends in part on their expectation of the money stock, M^e, and possibly on their expectations of government expenditures, g^e, and the level of taxes, t^e. Changes in these policy expectations induce changes in workers' price expectations and, in turn, induce variations in the position of the labor supply schedule. Therefore, at any given price level, equilibrium employment and real output, and thus the position of the aggregate supply schedule, vary with changes in anticipations of monetary and fiscal policy actions.

It follows that a fully anticipated monetary or fiscal policy action that causes the aggregate demand schedule to shift to the left also leads to a rightward shift in the aggregate supply schedule, as workers reduce their price expectations and increase their supply of labor. As a result, a fully anticipated monetary or fiscal policy action causes a rise in the equilibrium price level but has no effect on equilibrium real output. This conclusion corresponds to the new classical policy ineffectiveness proposition, which states that predictable, or systematic, monetary and fiscal policies cannot exert effects on real macroeconomic quantities.

For example, Figure 11 illustrates the effect of a reduction in the money stock that workers fully anticipate. The reduction in the actual quantity of money shifts the aggregate demand schedule leftward, while workers' reduction in their expectation of the money stock reduces their price-level expectation, causing the aggregate supply schedule to shift leftward. On net, equilibrium real output is unchanged.

Figure 11: The Effects of a Fully Anticipated Money Stock Reduction in the New Classical Model

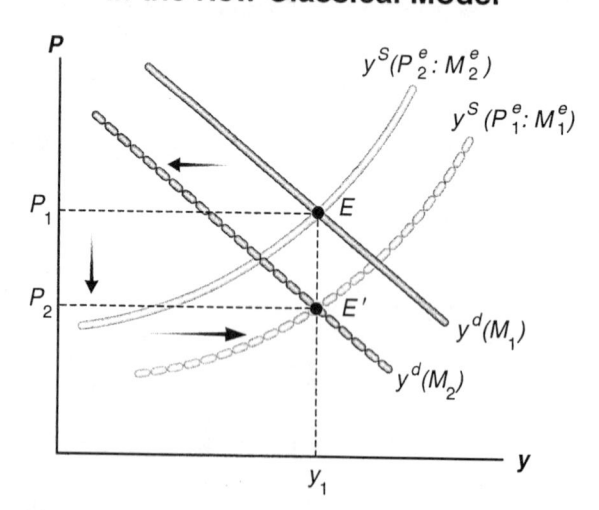

By way of contrast, unpredictable, or unsystematic, policy actions can cause short-term movements in employment and real output in the new classical model. Unanticipated monetary or fiscal policy actions cause the aggregate demand schedule to shift rightward. Because workers fail to anticipate the policies, however, their expectations do not change, and so the position of the aggregate supply schedule remains the same. Consequently, an rise in aggregate demand owing to an unexpected policy action can influence real macroeconomic variables, at least in the short run.

A key area in which economists have applied the rational expectations hypothesis in their efforts to understand how prices of financial market are determined. Proponents of efficient markets theory uses the rational expectations hypothesis to conclude that prices of financial assets should reflect all available information, including market participants' understanding of how financial markets determine asset prices. As a result, the efficient markets theory implies that the current price of a financial asset should reflect the rational forecast of the asset's returns. Failure of a financial asset price to reflect all such information would indicate inefficient functioning of a financial market, because traders could earn higher returns if they took into account information that is available to them. In efficient bond markets, there should be no unexploited opportunities for traders to earn higher returns, because if such opportunities existed, some traders would buy or sell more bonds, which would cause the market price of the bonds to change.

Economists often apply theory of efficient markets to markets for internationally traded bonds and national currencies. Currency exchange rates are determined by interactions between the forces of demand and supply in foreign exchange markets, which are the markets in which individuals, businesses, governments, and central banks exchange nations' currencies. Key determinants of the demand and supply of a nation's currency are that the desires of that nation's residents to import and the desires of foreign residents to purchase the nation's exports. The equilibrium exchange rate is the exchange rate at which the quantity of a nation's currency demanded in the foreign exchange market is equal to the quantity supplied.

The spot exchange rate, denoted S, is the rate of exchange for currencies to be traded immediately, or "on the spot." The forward exchange rate, F, is the market exchange rate on a forward currency contract that calls for delivery of a unit of a nation's currency in exchange for another at a predetermined price on a specified date. The quantity $(F - S)/S$ is called the forward discount, and the covered interest parity condition says that the interest rate on the bond of one nation should approximately equal the interest rate on another nation's bond that has the same term to maturity and other characteristics, plus the forward discount.

According to the uncovered interest parity condition, which applies to interest yields on bonds with identical risks and terms to maturity that are denominated in different national currencies, the yield on a bond denominated in a currency that is expected to depreciate must exceed another nation's bond yield by the rate at which the currency is expected to depreciate, plus a risk premium. In an efficient foreign exchange market, both covered and uncovered interest parity are satisfied simultaneously, which implies that the forward discount for one currency relative to a second currency is equal to the rate at which the first currency is expected to depreciate relative to the second currency plus a risk premium.

Key Terms and Concepts

Adaptive expectations
Covered interest parity
Efficient markets theory
Fed watching

Foreign exchange market efficiency
Foreign exchange markets
Forward currency contracts
Forward exchange rates
Policy ineffectiveness proposition
Rational expectations hypothesis
Spot exchange rate
Uncovered interest parity

Multiple-Choice Questions

1. Which of the following is involved in forming a purely adaptive expectation of the price level?

    I. past information
    II. current information
    III. an understanding of the workings of the economy

    A) I only
    B) II only
    C) both I and III
    D) I, II, and III

2. Which of the following is involved in forming a rational expectation of the price level?

    I. past information
    II. current information
    III. an understanding of the workings of the economy

    A) I only
    B) II only
    C) both I and III
    D) I, II, and III

3. Which of the following is not an example of an adaptive expectation?

    A) an expectation formed by averaging data over the past three years
    B) an expectation formed from a trend line of data for the past decade
    C) an expectation based on current information of a looming change in economic policymaking
    D) an expectation based on information relating to policy choices over a previous period of time

4. In contrast to the original classical theorists, the new classical macroeconomists assume that

A) people have perfect information and consequently form rational expectations.
B) people have imperfect information and but make use of rational expectations.
C) wages and prices are inflexible in the face of changes in economic conditions.
D) wages and prices adjust flexibly in response to changes in economic conditions.

5. In the new classical macroeconomic model,

I. information about the price level is incomplete.
II. inflation expectations are adaptive.
III. wages and prices are flexible.

A) I only
B) III only
C) both I and III
D) both II and III

6. According to the monetarist theory of the long run, the Phillips curve is vertical, so that monetary and fiscal policy actions cannot have permanent effects on the unemployment rate. The same is true of the new classical theory in the short run if people form

A) rational expectations and correctly anticipate monetary and fiscal policy actions.
B) adaptive expectations and partially anticipate monetary and fiscal policy actions.
C) rational expectations and fail to anticipate monetary and fiscal policy actions.
D) adaptive expectations and fail to anticipate monetary and fiscal policy actions.

7. According to the new classical macroeconomic model,

A) workers and firms fully anticipate actual changes in the price level.
B) workers and firms fully anticipate monetary and fiscal policy actions.
C) fully anticipated changes in the price level can change equilibrium real output.
D) fully anticipated monetary and fiscal policy actions do not affect equilibrium real output.

8. Within the new classical framework, a fully anticipated reduction in the nominal quantity of money in circulation causes

   A) a leftward shift of the aggregate demand schedule and a leftward shift of the aggregate supply schedule.
   B) a leftward shift of the aggregate demand schedule and a rightward shift of the aggregate supply schedule.
   C) a rightward shift of the aggregate demand schedule and a leftward shift of the aggregate supply schedule.
   D) a rightward shift of the aggregate demand schedule and a rightward shift of the aggregate supply schedule.

9. Consider the new classical theory of the market for real output. If people anticipate that a nation's central bank will increase the nominal money stock but it fails to do so, then the result will be

   A) a rise in the price level and a decline in real output.
   B) a rise in the price level and a rise in real output.
   C) a fall in the price level and a rise in real output.
   D) no change in the price level or in real output.

10. According to the new classical theory, an increase in the nominal money stock that is unanticipated in the short run can induce

    I. a short-run increase in the price level.
    II. a long-run reduction in unemployment.
    III. a short-run increase in real output.

    A) I only
    B) II only
    C) both I and III
    D) both II and III

11. The new classical model implies that monetary policy secrecy

    I. contributes to the potential for monetary policy actions to influence real output.
    II. likely makes real output more volatile than it otherwise would be.
    III. is required for monetary policy actions to stabilize inflation.

    A) I only
    B) III only
    C) both I and II
    D) both II and III

12. In an efficient market,

    I. prices reflect all available information.
    II. actual prices always equal expected prices.
    III. actual amounts traded always equal expected trading volumes.

    A) I only
    B) III only
    C) both I and II
    D) both II and III

13. According to the theory of efficient markets,

    A) financial market speculators can never profit from new information.
    B) speculative profits from new information should be short-lived.
    C) the price of a financial asset fails to reflect new information.
    D) financial asset prices and profits never vary over time.

14. If U.S. residents increase their desired purchases of Brazilian goods at the same time that Brazilian residents reduce their desired purchases of U.S. goods, then if exchange rates float and other factors are unchanged,

    A) the value of the U.S. dollar relative to the Brazilian real will decline.
    B) the value of the U.S. dollar relative to the Brazilian real will increase.
    C) the U.S. dollar and Brazilian real both will depreciate relative to other nations' currencies.
    D) the U.S. dollar and Brazilian real both will appreciate relative to other nations' currencies.

15. Suppose that the rate of exchange of British pounds for Japanese yen is measured in terms of pounds per yen. If there is a rise in the demand for yen by British residents, then the result in the foreign exchange market would be

    A) an excess quantity of yen supplied at the initial equilibrium exchange rate that would lead to a rise in the equilibrium exchange rate.
    B) an excess quantity of yen supplied at the initial equilibrium exchange rate that would lead to a fall in the equilibrium exchange rate.
    C) an excess quantity of yen demanded at the initial equilibrium exchange rate that would lead to a fall in the equilibrium exchange rate.
    D) an excess quantity of yen demanded at the initial equilibrium exchange rate that would lead to a rise in the equilibrium exchange rate.

16. In the foreign exchange market, a rise in the supply of U.S. dollars in exchange for European Monetary Union (EMU) euros would cause

    I. an appreciation of the EMU euro relative to the U.S. dollar.
    II. an increase in the exchange rate expressed in terms of U.S. dollars per EMU euro.
    III. a reduction in the exchange rate expressed in terms of EMU euros per U.S. dollar.

    A) both I and II only
    B) both I and III only
    C) both II and III only
    D) I, II, and III

17. Based solely on the covered interest parity condition, if the forward rate of exchange expressed in U.S. dollars per European Monetary Union (EMU) euro exceeds the spot rate of exchange expressed in U.S. dollars per EMU euro, then

    A) the interest rate on an EMU bond will exceed the interest rate on a U.S. bond that has the same characteristics and an identical term to maturity.
    B) the interest rate on a U.S. bond will exceed the interest rate on an EMU bond that has the same characteristics and an identical term to maturity.
    C) foreign exchange market traders anticipate that the U.S. dollar will appreciate relative to the EMU euro.
    D) foreign exchange market traders anticipate that the EMU euro will appreciate relative to the U.S. dollar.

18. Based solely on the uncovered interest parity condition, if the interest rate on a Russian bond exceeds the interest rate on a European Monetary Union (EMU) bond with the same term to maturity, then if there is no risk premium,

    A) the forward exchange rate expressed in EMU euros per Russian rubles exceeds the spot exchange rate expressed in EMU euros per Russian ruble.
    B) the forward exchange rate expressed in EMU euros per Russian rubles is less than the spot exchange rate expressed in EMU euros per Russian ruble.
    C) foreign exchange market traders anticipate that the EMU euro will appreciate relative to the Russian ruble.
    D) foreign exchange market traders anticipate that the Russian ruble will appreciate relative to the EMU euro.

19. If foreign exchange markets are efficient, then if there is no risk premium and the interest rate on Canadian bonds is less than the interest rate on Mexican bonds with the same term to maturity,

   I. foreign exchange market traders anticipate that the Canadian dollar will appreciate relative to the Mexican peso in the future.
   II. foreign exchange market traders anticipate that the spot exchange rate expressed in terms of Mexican pesos per Canadian dollar will increase in the future.
   III. the forward exchange rate expressed in terms of Mexican pesos per Canadian dollar exceeds the spot exchange rate expressed in terms of Mexican pesos per Canadian dollar.

   A) both I and II only
   B) both I and III only
   C) both II and III only
   D) I, II, and III

20. In an efficient foreign exchange market, in the absence of a risk premium,

   A) the forward premium is always equal to zero.
   B) the forward premium equals the expected rate of currency depreciation.
   D) the expected rate of depreciation for a nation's currency must exceed zero.
   D) the expected rate of depreciation for a nation's currency always equals zero.

Short-Answer Questions

1. What is an adaptive expectation?

2. What is a rational expectation?

3. What is the policy ineffectiveness proposition?

4. What would constitute a "representative-agent" model of the economy?

5. What is the term that describes the process of carefully observing a central bank in an effort to improve upon forecasts of its policies?

6. If the current market price of a good, service, or financial asset fails to take into account all information available to buyers and sellers, then what can we say about this market?

7. What is a forward exchange rate?

8. What condition holds if the interest rate on a bond issued in one nation exceeds the interest rate on a foreign bond with the same term to maturity and other characteristics by the amount of the forward premium or discount?

9. What condition holds if the interest rate on a bond issued in one nation exceeds the interest rate on a foreign bond with the same term to maturity and other characteristics by the amount of anticipated depreciation of the nation's currency?

10. What condition is met if foreign exchange markets are efficient?

Chapter 12: Rational Wage Stickiness — Modern Keynesian Theory with Rational Expectations

Chapter Summary

Modern Keynesian theory uses the rational expectations hypothesis in models of inflexible wages and prices. According to this approach, workers and firms agree to contracts that set the terms, such as wages and benefits, that govern the employment of workers with firms over a given time period. These contracts rule out instantaneous adjustments of expectations to monetary policy actions, allowing for the possibility that monetary policy can have real effects even if people form inflation expectations rationally.

The modern Keynesian theorists offer three possible rationales for nominal wage contracts. One is that using such contracts saves firms and workers from incurring the labor-market transaction costs entailed in continuously conducting new auctions of workers' skills when labor demand and supply conditions go through temporary variations. Another rationale for nominal wage contracts is risk aversion. If market wages were to rise unexpectedly, then workers would be better off while firms would not, whereas if market wages were to fall unexpectedly, firms would be better off while workers would not. Hence, workers and firms may agree to fix the wage in advance, thereby shielding themselves from risks that they otherwise might face if wages were market-determined. The third rationale for nominal wage contracts is asymmetric information, or possession of information by workers (or firms) that is not available to firms (or workers). Wage contracts could represent a means by which both workers and firms might seek to stem difficulties that could arise from asymmetric information.

In the modern Keynesian contracting model, the shared goal of workers and firms when they negotiate a contract wage for contract interval is to try to achieve the same equilibrium wage and employment level that they anticipate will arise in during that interval if labor-market equilibrium were to occur. Workers and firms do not know the precise conditions that will prevail during the contract interval, but they attempt to forecast the full-information nominal wage rate that they expect that the classical labor auction market would have yielded during the contract period. This is the wage at which they anticipate that the labor demand schedule will cross the labor supply schedule during that interval. If the price level turns out to be higher than workers and firms had anticipated when they negotiated their contracts, then the value of labor's marginal product also would be higher than expected at the time the wage was negotiated. Thus, firms would demand more labor than they had anticipated, and workers would provide more labor services and produce more output at the contract wage than they had expected. As a result, an unexpected increase in the price level leads to a rise in real output, so the aggregate supply schedule slopes upward in the basic modern Keynesian model.

Even though the modern Keynesian theory assumed that contracts make the nominal wage rate sticky, the theory is based on the rational expectations hypothesis used by new classical economists. Like the new classical theory, the modern Keynesian theory also predicts that the short-run aggregate supply schedule slopes upward because an unanticipated price-level decrease induces a decline in real output.

Furthermore, the modern Keynesian theory indicates that if workers and firms fully anticipate monetary and fiscal policies that will be enacted during the terms of wage contracts, the policies will have no effects on real output. For example, the Figure 12 illustrates the effects of a reduction in the quantity of money that workers and firms are able to anticipate before concluding wage negotiations. If the nominal wage initially contracted by workers and firms was equal to W_1^C and if the initial money stock was equal to M_1, then the equilibrium price level and volume of real output would be determined at point E. A reduction in the money stock shifts aggregate demand to the left and pushes down the equilibrium price level. If workers and firms correctly anticipate this contractionary policy action, however, they reduce the contracted nominal wage, causing the aggregate supply schedule to shift rightward. On net, equilibrium real output remains the same.

Figure 12: The Effects of a Money Stock Reduction that Workers and Firms Fully Anticipate in the Modern Keynesian Contracting Model

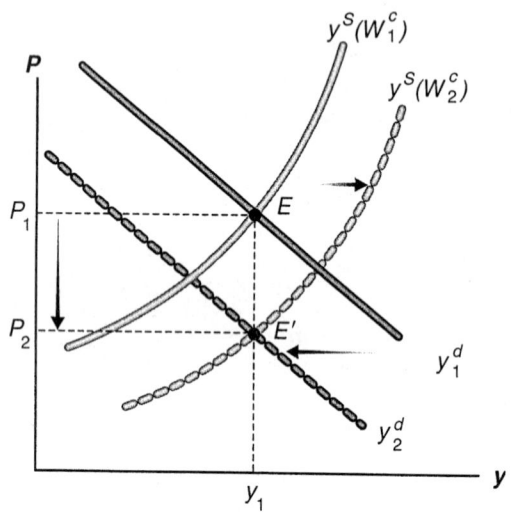

This similarity between the basic predictions of the new classical and modern Keynesian theories is called observational equivalence. Economists interested in determining which theory has greater relevance have begun by seeking to determine whether real output and employment do really respond only to price level misperceptions, as both theories predict. They also have sought to identify aspects of the modern Keynesian theory of wage contracting that distinguish it more clearly from the new classical approach, to see if the two theories make separate predictions that might indicate which theory does a better job of explaining real-world outcomes.

Wage contracts sometimes require automatic adjustment of wages during the interval in which the contract has been binding, via what are called cost-of-living-adjustment (COLA) clauses. COLA contracts set a base wage that creates a floor on workers' earnings but nevertheless specify additional wage payments in the event of inflation. Hence, COLA contracts are examples wage indexation, in which contracted wages are "indexed," or adjusted automatically to changes in the price level. If all wages in the economy specify fully proportionate and continuous adjustment of the wage to increases or decreases in the price level, then the aggregate supply schedule is vertical, as in the classical model. Full indexation thereby makes equilibrium real output less stable in the face of volatility of relative prices of key resources such as oil or sudden technological changes that can cause the position of the aggregate supply schedule to vary. Nevertheless, full indexation makes equilibrium real output insensitive to variations in aggregate demand. This suggests that aggregate wage indexation should decline if aggregate demand variability declines relative to variability in aggregate supply.

The optimal length of a nominal wage contract depends in part on the total cost of negotiating the contract, which is the sum of the opportunity cost of the time spent in contract negotiations and the direct costs incurred in this process. As the total cost of contract negotiation increases, the duration of a typical contract should also rise, as workers and firms postpone incurring contract negotiation costs. Nevertheless, by lengthening the term of a wage contract, workers and firms increase the period over which they must try to anticipate factors that could cause the price level to vary. This exposes them to adverse effects of variability in the full-information wage and employment level that result from volatility in the positions of the aggregate demand and aggregate supply schedules. Hence, greater variability of aggregate demand and aggregate supply reduces the optimal contract length.

Because workers and firms make their own decisions about the timing of contract negotiations, dates that contracts begin and end tend be staggered, meaning that they begin on different dates. Staggering of contracts and differences in the contract durations across the economy leads to contract overlapping. As a result, portion of workers and firms in the economy with contracts that set wages at earlier dates are more limited in their ability to respond quickly to systematic policy changes. This implies that the effects of both anticipated and unanticipated policy actions on employment and real output can be longer lasting than predicted by the new classical model. Thus, a key prediction of modern Keynesian theory is greater persistence in policy-induced business-cycle recessions or expansions. Contract synchronization, or identical timing of contracts, would ensure that all workers and firms have the same information as they anticipate conditions during the coming contract period, thereby limiting persistence in business cycles to the common interval of all the synchronized contracts. Nonetheless, overlapping contracts help to mute responses of the aggregate wage to changes in aggregate demand conditions, thereby limiting the size of wage changes and the effects that they ultimately may have on the price level and on the sizes of business-cycle downturns.

Critics of modern Keynesian theory argue that some basic predictions of contract-based theories do not do a good job of fitting the facts. They point out that if the contract-based theories are correct, then rises in the price level induced by increases in aggregate demand should cause real wages to decline, so that real wages should move counter-cyclically. In fact, many studies of the overall behavior of real wages in the United States have found that real wages tend to move pro-cyclically, rising during business-cycle expansions and falling during business-cycle contractions. They also point out that modern Keynesian theory also indicates that significant variability in aggregate demand relative to variability in aggregate supply should induce workers and firms to increase the extent of wage indexation, yet the use of COLA clauses in the United States has not always risen during periods of highly volatile aggregate demand or of low variability in aggregate supply. Finally, they argue that the decline in unionization of the U.S. labor force makes contract-based theories less relevant.

Proponents of contract-based theories have responded that studies of the cyclical behavior of the aggregate real wage are very sensitive to how wages are averaged and to the frequency of the data that one analyzes and that contract wages theoretically are countercyclical only if all other factors are held constant. In addition, they point out that after controlling for changes in other factors that influence contracted wages, observed patterns in real wages are still consistent with the predictions of the contract-based theory. Furthermore, those who favor the contract-based approach have responded by conducting more refined studies that indicate that apparent failures of the modern Keynesian theory may have stemmed from measurement problems and imperfectly constructed tests of the theory's implications. Others have sought to make the basic contracting theory more realistic by taking into account the effects of changing competition among U.S. firms and increased competition from abroad. Greater competition has certainly increased the flexibility of nominal wages in a larger portion of the U.S. economy. This has led some modern Keynesian theorists to imbed contracting theories in multisector models that admit the existence of a variety of individuals, markets, and industries. These multisector models predict that real wages will be countercyclical in sectors of the economy in which wage contracts are important but procyclical in other sectors, thereby potentially explaining why the behavior of aggregate real wage and price levels for the economy as a whole seems to be both partially consistent and partially inconsistent with predictions of both theories. Multisector models also may help to explain which it might be difficult for policymakers to identify policy actions that would stabilize all parts of the economy simultaneously.

Key Terms and Concepts

Asymmetric information
Cost-of-Living-Adjustment (COLA) clauses
Multisector models
Observational equivalence
Wage indexation

Multiple-Choice Questions

1. Which of the following is not a commonly cited rationale for the existence of contracts that fix workers' nominal wages?

   A) high inflation expectations of workers
   B) significant risk aversion on the part of workers
   C) large transaction costs of auctioning workers' skills
   D) asymmetric information about workers' skills and effort

2. According to the modern Keynesian theory of nominal wage stickiness,

   I. workers form adaptive expectations of the price level during a contract interval.
   II. firms form rational expectations of the price level during a contract interval.
   III. the level of employment is determined by the position of the labor supply schedule.

   A) I only
   B) II only
   C) both I and III
   D) both II and III

3. According to the modern Keynesian theory of nominal wage stickiness,

   I. the base contract wage is equal to the expected wage that would equate the quantities of labor supplied and demanded during the contract interval.
   II. a rise in real output caused by an increase in aggregate demand should be accompanied by a decline in the real wage.
   III. a reduction in the price level caused by a fall in aggregate demand should be accompanied by a decline in the real wage.

   A) I only
   B) III only
   C) both I and II
   D) both II and III

4. Which one of the following statements is true within the context of the modern Keynesian contracting theory?

   A) Nominal wage inflexibility implies that the aggregate real wage is rigid over time.
   B) Nominal wage inflexibility leads to procyclical behavior of aggregate real wages.
   C) Real output increases in response to a rise in the contracted nominal wage.
   D) Real output increases in response to an unexpected rise in the price level.

5. Within the context of the modern Keynesian contracting theory, unemployment might result from

   A) an unexpected decline in the price level relative to the value that workers and firms had anticipated would arise during the term of a wage contract.
   B) an unexpected rise in real output relative to the level that workers and firms had anticipated would arise during the term of a wage contract.
   C) an increase in the rate of inflation that workers and firms had anticipated when they established a base contract wage.
   D) a rise in the level of output that workers and firms had anticipated when they established a base contract wage.

6. The fact that the basic modern Keynesian contracting theory and the new classical theory both predict that real output varies in response to price-level misperceptions is called

   A) analytical equivalence, and this fact leads to a vertical aggregate supply schedule in both theories.
   B) observational equivalence, and this fact leads to an upward-sloping aggregate supply schedule in both theories.
   C) rational expectations equivalence, and this fact implies that unemployment stems from anticipated inflation in both theories.
   D) representative-agent equivalence, and this fact implies that unemployment stems from unexpected inflation in both theories.

7. If workers and firms agree to contracts that fully index nominal wages to changes in the price level, then

   I. the aggregate supply schedule is vertical.
   II. the real wage does not change when the price level rises.
   III. employment is determined by the position of the labor supply schedule.

   A) I only
   B) III only
   C) both I and II
   D) both II and III

8. If the aggregate real wage moves countercyclically, then

   A) an aggregate demand expansion leads to no change in the aggregate real wage.
   B) an aggregate demand expansion leads to a rise in the aggregate real wage.
   C) an aggregate demand contraction leads to a fall in the aggregate real wage.
   D) an aggregate demand contraction leads to a rise in the aggregate real wage.

9. If unexpected shifts in the position of the aggregate supply schedule are commonplace, then

   A) full indexation of nominal wages to unexpected price-level changes stabilizes equilibrium real output.
   B) full indexation of nominal wages to unexpected price-level changes destabilizes equilibrium real output.
   C) failure to index nominal wages to unexpected variations in the price level leads to a permanently lower natural level of real output.
   D) failure to index nominal wages to unexpected variations in the price level leads to a permanently higher natural level of real output.

10. In the absence of any indexation of nominal wages to unexpected changes in the price level,

   I. the aggregate supply schedule is vertical.
   II. the aggregate real wage is invariant in the face of variations in the position of the aggregate demand schedule.
   III. equilibrium real output is less stable, as compared with fully indexed wages, in the face of variations in the position of the aggregate demand schedule.

   A) I only
   B) III only
   C) both I and II
   D) both II and III

11. If equilibrium real output increases in the face of an unexpected rise in the price level, then we may conclude that this observation offers support for the conclusion that

   A) the aggregate supply schedule may be horizontal, ruling out the possibility that nominal wages may be partly indexed to inflation.
   B) the modern Keynesian theory is correct, but we can rule out the possibility that the new classical theory is correct.
   C) either the aggregate supply schedule may be vertical, or nominal wages may be completely indexed to inflation.
   D) either the modern Keynesian theory is correct, or the new classical theory is correct.

12. Consider a nation in which a federation of trade unions negotiates wages on behalf of all the nation's workers. A top official of the federation receives inside information that the nation's central bank intends to increase the growth of the nominal money stock during the interval in which the next year's national labor contracts will be in force. If the federation official communicates this information to those currently bargaining with firms concerning the base wage for the next year's labor contracts, then if all other factors with the exception of the higher money growth rate next year are unchanged from the current year, then the modern Keynesian contract theory predicts that

   I. the base wage for next year's labor contracts should increase relative to the base wage for the current year's contracts.
   II. the position of the aggregate supply schedule should unambiguously shift to the left during the next year.
   III. the equilibrium level of real output should unambiguously increase during the next year.

   A) I only
   B) III only
   C) both I and II
   D) both II and III

13. Suppose that a nation has synchronized wage contracts that are not indexed to inflation. Results of a decline in aggregate demand for workers and firms that negotiated these contracts would be

   A) unexpected declines in employment, real output, and the price level.
   B) unexpected increases in employment, real output, and the price level.
   C) an unexpected fall in employment and a leftward shift in the position of the aggregate supply schedule.
   D) an unexpected rise in employment and a rightward shift in the position of the aggregate supply schedule.

14. As compared with a setting in which nonindexed wage contracts are synchronized, a setting with staggered, overlapping, and nonindexed wage contracts will

   A) imply a fixed level of real output and a highly variable price level.
   B) imply no significant distinctions for real output and the price level.
   C) lead to more persistence in real output movements and the consequent potential for greater real output stability.
   D) lead to less persistence in real output movements and, as a result, less stability of aggregate real output over a given business cycle.

15. Which of the following would contribute to a shortening of the interval of a contract that fixes the nominal wage?

    I. greater variability in the position of the aggregate demand schedule
    II. greater variability in the position of the aggregate supply schedule
    III. higher transactions costs entailed in negotiating wage contracts

    A) I only
    B) III only
    C) both I and II
    D) both II and III

16. Assuming that all other factors are unchanged, which one of the following statements would be true if the position of the aggregate demand schedule became more variable with the passage of time?

    A) If workers and firms negotiate nominal wage contracts, then the optimal durations of these contracts would decline over time.
    B) If nominal wage contracts contain no provision for wage indexation, then the aggregate real output level would become more stable over time.
    C) If nominal wage contracts specify complete wage indexation, then the aggregate real output level would vary to a greater extent over time.
    D) If contracts at various industries have the same durations but are staggered, the real wages at those industries that first negotiated their contracts would be more variable than those with later contract negotiation dates.

17. Assuming that all other factors are unchanged, which one of the following statements would be true if the position of the aggregate supply schedule became more variable with the passage of time?

    A) If nominal wage contracts contain no provision for wage indexation, then the aggregate real output level would be unaffected.
    B) If workers and firms negotiate nominal wage contracts, then the optimal durations of these contracts would rise over time.
    C) If nominal wage contracts specify complete wage indexation, then the aggregate real output level would vary to a greater extent over time.
    D) If contracts at various industries have the same durations but are staggered, the real wages at those industries that first negotiated their contracts would be more variable than those with later contract negotiation dates.

18. If nominal wages are completely indexed in all wage contracts, then which one of the following statements would be incorrect?

    A) The aggregate supply schedule would be vertical.
    B) The aggregate real wage would move countercyclically.
    C) Real output would vary in the face of shifts in the aggregate supply schedule.
    D) Real output would be stable in the face of shifts in the aggregate demand schedule.

19. Which of the following statements is supported by U.S. experience?

    I. The extent of wage indexation has increased in recent years.
    II. The extent to which workers are unionized has declined in recent years.
    III. The degree of overall competition in markets for goods and services has declined in recent years.

    A) I only
    B) II only
    C) both I and III
    D) both II and III

20. Which of the following are key features of multisector macroeconomic models that distinguish them from other theories?

    I. Such models, in contrast to other modern Keynesian models, allow for overlapping contracts and persistent movements in real output.
    II. Real wages might move countercyclically in sectors with wage contracts even though the aggregate real wage moves pro-cyclically.
    III. Monetary and fiscal policies might be unable to stabilize all sectors of a nation's economy simultaneously.

    A) I only
    B) II only
    C) both I and III
    D) both II and III

Short-Answer Questions

1. In macroeconomics, what is the meaning of the term "observational equivalence"?

2. Under what types of contracts are nominal wages indexed to inflation in the United States?

3. What is real-wage procyclicality?

4. What is real-wage countercyclicality?

5. In the modern Keynesian contracting theory, what is the value of a base nominal wage determined in a typical contract?

6. What are synchronized wage contracts?

7. What are overlapping wage contracts?

8. How does an increase in the variability of aggregate demand affect the optimal duration of a nonindexed nominal wage contract?

9. How does a reduction in the variability of aggregate supply affect the optimal duration of a nonindexed nominal wage contract?

10. What is a multisector macroeconomic model?

Chapter 13: Market Failures versus Perfect Markets — New Keynesians versus Real-Business-Cycle Theorists

Chapter Summary

Macroeconomists have developed further theories despite the fact that the rational expectations hypothesis is intuitively appealing and makes macroeconomic models internally consistent. One key reason for this is that current theories have trouble explaining persistence in employment and real output movements, such as the Great Depression of the 1930s. The experience during this period conflicted with he new classical theory's implication that predictable policy actions should note have long-lived effects on employment and real output. Although the modern Keynesian theory with staggered and overlapping contracts might seem to help in explaining persistent effects of a sizable decline in aggregate demand such as that of the 1930s, unions and explicit contracts were not widespread features of U.S. labor markets until the latter part of the period. More recently, techniques that economists developed during the 1980s for examining time series, or data recorded over successive periods of time, indicated that temporary changes in economic conditions often have had long-lasting effects on real GDP even in years beyond the Great Depression. Yet most macroeconomic theories indicated that such temporary changes should simply result in short-lived GDP fluctuations

New Keynesian theories attempt to explain business cycle persistence and long-lasting periods of high unemployment via theories that clearly explain price or wage stickiness without appeal to explicit contracts. Some new Keynesian theories, therefore, seek to develop models in which sluggishness in price adjustments, or price inertia, is a central feature. One common element of these theories is the assumption of imperfect competition, or markets in which there are limited numbers of buyers or sellers, barriers to market entry or exit exist, or consumers and differentiate among firm products or factor services may be differentiated. Another common element is the possibility of market failure, or the failure of a private market to reach an equilibrium that reflects all the costs and benefits entailed in producing a good or in providing a factor service, often because of the existence of externalities, or situations in which a private cost or benefit differs from a social cost or benefit because of spillover effects stemming from the production or consumption of a good or service. At an aggregate level, macroeconomic externalities can occur, meaning that are situations can arise in which most markets in the economy may achieve equilibrium positions that fail to account for spillovers, so that equilibrium aggregate real output, employment, and the price level all differ from their long-run, natural levels.

According to the new Keynesian small-menu-cost theory, imperfect competition and macroeconomic externalities may explain price inertia and the persistent response of real output to temporary business-cycle variations. This theory is similar to the earlier administered pricing hypothesis advanced during the 1930s, which proposed that firms that imperfectly competitive firms may be able to maintain inflexible prices for relatively long periods. The small-menu-cost theory assumes that firms incur small but measurable costs when they change the prices of their products. Although firms achieve profit gains if they respond to altered market conditions by changing their prices, this gain typically is small relative to total profits and potentially could be smaller than the small menu costs that the firms face. As a result, firms could choose to leave their prices unchanged. This would require them to change their output by a larger amount than they otherwise would in light of changed market conditions. Decisions by some firms to cut their prices also could have spillover effects onto those firms that do not change their prices, and *vice versa*. In this way, macroeconomic externalities could arise that could cause business cycles to occur and to persist. Critics of the small-menu-cost theory point out that the profit gain from changing prices lasts for many periods and in total might easily outweigh a one-time small menu cost, making the empirical relevance of the theory open to question. They also question the presumption that firms face costs in changing prices but not in changing output.

Efficiency wage models and the insider-outsider theory are new Keynesian theories of persistent unemployment. According to the efficiency wage model, imperfectly competitive firms may choose to pay their workers real wages above the wages implied by purely competitive behavior, in an effort to maintain high employee morale and spur greater worker productivity. As a result, a labor surplus, or unemployment, can arise. According to the insider-outsider theory, current employees (insiders) of a firm may have an advantage in maintaining their jobs and wages, perhaps because their employer regards expenses on their training as a form of capital investment, thereby imposing barriers on the firm's ability to hire others (outsiders) who otherwise would be willing to work at a lower real wage. The result would be persistent, involuntary unemployment for outsiders.

A common element of complete new Keynesian models is coordination failure, or the inability of workers and firms to plan and implement labor supply, production, and pricing decisions because of macroeconomic externalities that have different effects on heterogeneous workers and firms. Heterogeneity might arise from size differences, cost differences, product differentiation, different tastes and preferences, or differing information. As a result of worker and firm heterogeneities, strategic interactions, or the interdependence of economic choices that people make as individuals or together with others, may exist. This requires economists to apply game theory, or the theory of how people make decisions in light of strategic interactions, to analyze the equilibrium choices that households and firms make. To do this, economists must consider the possibility of noncooperative behavior, in which each household or firm does the best it can to look out for its own interests irrespective of the interests of other households or firms, or of cooperative behavior, in which households and firms work together to achieve their common good. More than one equilibrium can arise when households and firms behave noncooperatively, which leads to the possibility of either high- or low-level equilibrium positions for the economy. A proposed new Keynesian rationale for activist policymaking is to overcome coordination failures and thereby move the economy from a low-level equilibrium to a high-level equilibrium.

An alternative to the new Keynesian approach is real-business-cycle theory, which emphasizes the importance of real factors, such as technological or productivity change, as elements that induce cyclical fluctuations in economic activity. There are two key features that real-business-cycle models share. One is that they are equilibrium models in which wages always adjust to equate the quantity of labor demanded with the quantity of labor supplied and in which prices always move to equilibrate the desired purchases of goods and services with the amount of goods and services supplied. The other is that real-business-cycle models are dynamic models intended describe how macroeconomic variables move over time. In many ways, real-business-cycle models have the same basic policy implications as the classical model. Real business cycle theory differs from the classical model, however, in its treatment of money and the effects of monetary policy. Whereas the classical model assumes that the nominal money stock is fully controlled by a central bank, in the real business cycle theory the nominal quantity of money supply is determined largely by interactions between the depository financial institutions and the public. When real income rises, people increase their demand for transactions services from banks, thereby raising the total amount of bank deposit money, or inside money, which therefore has no causal effects on any macroeconomic variables, including the price level. Only outside money, which is composed of currency and bank reserves that a central bank can control because they are determined by the central bank's policies, can affect the price level.

Figure 13 shows how the real-business-cycle theory explains most variations in real output over time. In panel (a), a reduction in the productivity of labor causes the aggregate production to rotate downward, thereby inducing real output to decline from one period to the next. Afterward, however, an increase in labor productivity results in a real-output expansion. As shown in panel (b), the result is cyclical variations in real output.

Figure 13: A Real Business Cycle

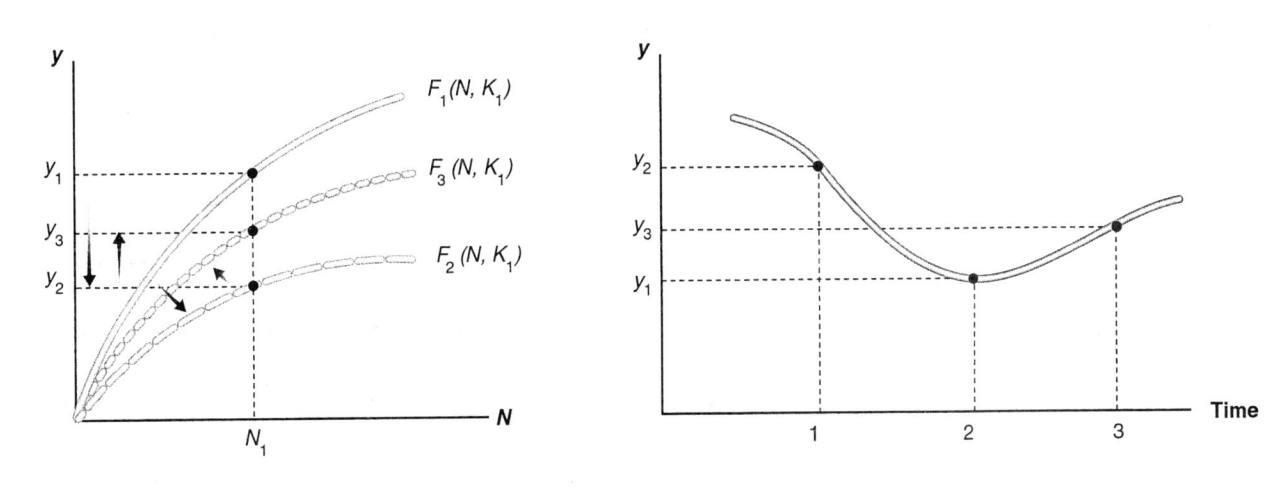

A controversial aspect of real-business-cycle theory has been its emphasis on inductive theory in which economists draw general conclusion from reference to observed data, and its de-emphasis of deductive theory in which economists make a prediction about real-world outcomes based on a theoretical model. Instead of using standard statistical tests to evaluate how well real-world data correspond to deductive predictions, real-business-cycle theorists often use calibration techniques. This approach entails three steps. First, real-business-cycle theorists use estimates of elasticities and specific data estimates from previous statistical studies directly in their theoretical models. Second, they use computers to calculate how these variables would change over time within the models that they construct. Finally, they compare the cyclical properties of their artificially created data with those of real-world data. Real-business-cycle theorists call this general approach quantitative theory, or the use of numerical calculations to develop theoretical models that fit observed business-cycle facts.

Together, the main contributions of the new Keynesian and real-business-cycle theories have been their focus on the potential importance of heterogeneities, the possible usefulness of game theory in macroeconomic analysis, renewed attention to the role that supply-side factors may play in business cycles, and a recognition that business cycles and economic growth may be related phenomena. It remains to be seen which, if either, body of recent theory will prove more successful in helping economists make predictions and develop policy prescriptions.

Key Terms and Concepts

Administered pricing hypothesis
Calibration
Cooperative behavior
Coordination failures
Deduction
Dynamic models
Efficiency wage theory
Externality
Induction
Inside money
Insider-outsider theory
Macroeconomic externalities
Market failure
Noncooperative behavior
Outside money
Price inertia
Quantitative theory
Real-business-cycle theory
Real business cycle theory
Small menu costs
Strategic interactions
Time series

Multiple-Choice Questions

1. Which of the following is an example of time series data?

    I. data on the components of GDP during the peak of a business cycle
    II. 2004 real wage data for people of various ages
    III. GDP data spanning the period since 1959

    A) I only
    B) III only
    C) both I and II
    D) both II and III

2. Based on estimates of the degree of price inertia discussed in the text, which one of the following nations experienced the greatest price inertia since the 1950s?

    A) Japan
    B) Germany
    C) the United States
    D) the United Kingdom

3. The Great Depression of the 1930s remains a puzzle to macroeconomists, because

    A) real GDP was so slow to adjust during that decade.
    B) employment was so slow to adjust during that decade.
    C) the downturn in real GDP and employment during that decade was so deep and lasted such a long time.
    D) the downturn in real GDP and employment during that decade was not accompanied by any change in the price level.

4. What is the term for a situation in which the number of buyers or sellers is limited, there are barriers to market entry or exit, and firm products or factor services are differentiated?

    A) imperfect competition
    B) coordination failure
    C) pure competition
    D) market failure

5. What is the term for situation in which a private interaction among buyers and sellers does not permit them to reach an equilibrium that reflects all the costs and benefits entailed in producing a good or in providing a factor service?

A) imperfect competition
B) coordination failure
C) pure competition
D) market failure

6. Which of the following would constitute a macroeconomic externality?

A) The sale of large car stereo speakers to a teenager creates noise that bothers his neighbors.
B) The interactions among the bulk of firms and consumers creates price rigidities that influence the behavior of the unemployment rate.
C) The existence of small menu costs at a large company induces the company to maintain an unchanged price list even as its competitors vary their prices.
D) An imperfectly competitive firm pays its workers a higher real wage to boost employee morale even as its competitors continue to hold the line on wage increases.

7. Which of the following is an example of a small menu cost?

I. expenses entailed in printing new catalogs of product prices
II. costs incurred in renegotiating pricing agreements with customers
III. costs incurred in conducting managerial meetings to determine new product prices

A) both I and II only
B) both I and III only
C) both II and III only
D) I, II, and III

8. The key idea of small-menu-cost models of price stickiness is that

A) the profit gain from changing a firm's price may be less than the cost that the firm incurs as a result of a price change.
B) the profit gain from changing a firm's price may be greater than the cost that the firm incurs as a result of a price change.
C) higher costs associated with price changes may conflict with a firm's efforts to keep its total operating costs as low as possible.
D) higher costs associated with price changes may conflict with a firm's efforts to keep real wages high in an effort to promote higher worker productivity.

9. Which of the following is a criticism of small-menu-cost models?

   I. There may be output-adjustment costs as well as costs associated with changing prices.
   II. The profit loss from keeping prices unchanged in the face of a change in product demand is very large relative to total profits.
   III. The profit loss from keeping prices unchanged in the face of a change in product demand lasts for longer than the period in which a firm incurs a cost of changing its price.

   A) I only
   B) II only
   C) both I and III
   D) both II and III

10. The new Keynesian hypothesis that the productivity of workers depends on the real wage rate and that imperfectly competitive firms respond to this relationship by employing fewer workers is called

    A) the small-menu-cost theory.
    B) the insider-outsider theory.
    C) wage productivity theory.
    D) efficiency wage theory.

11. The fundamental prediction of efficiency wage theory is that

    A) price stickiness can result from efforts by firms to keep real wages at levels that boost employee productivity, thereby pushing up the firms' operating costs.
    B) unemployment can result from efforts by firms to keep real wages at levels that boost employee productivity, thereby creating a surplus in the labor market.
    C) price stickiness can result from efforts by employed workers to develop artificial barriers to the employment of qualified workers who currently do not have jobs.
    D) unemployment can result from efforts by employed workers to develop artificial barriers to the employment of qualified workers who currently do not have jobs.

12. The fundamental prediction of the insider-outsider model is that

    A) price stickiness can result from efforts by firms to keep real wages at levels that boost employee productivity, thereby pushing up the firms' operating costs.
    B) unemployment can result from efforts by firms to keep real wages at levels that boost employee productivity, thereby creating a surplus in the labor market.
    C) price stickiness can result from efforts by employed workers to develop artificial barriers to the employment of qualified workers who currently do not have jobs.
    D) unemployment can result from efforts by employed workers to develop artificial barriers to the employment of qualified workers who currently do not have jobs.

13. According to the new Keynesian theory, which of the following could account for heterogeneity among individuals and firms, which in turn might help give rise to coordination failures?

    I. product differentiation
    II. differences in production costs
    III. differential levels of knowledge about economic conditions

    A) both I and II only
    B) both I and III only
    C) both II and III only
    D) I, II, and III

14. If an individual does the best that she can to pursue her own interests irrespective of the interests of others, then this individual engages in

    A) heterogeneous coordination.
    B) noncooperative behavior.
    C) cooperative behavior.
    D) a coordination failure.

15. In contrast to other macroeconomic models, dynamic models

    A) describe how macroeconomic variables vary in response to shocks.
    B) describe how macroeconomic variables change with the passage of time.
    C) explain why macroeconomic variables change when coordination failures take place.
    D) explain why macroeconomic variables vary in response to microeconomic factors.

17. What form of money depends on conditions within the banking system, thereby adjusting automatically to changing economic conditions without any action by a central bank?

   A) inside money
   B) outside money
   C) circulating currency
   D) reserves banks hold with the central bank

16. According to the real-business-cycle theory, which of the following could account for a business-cycle downturn?

   I. a decline in the quantity of money in circulation
   II. a significant decline in real government expenditures
   III. a reduced ability to use factors of production in the most cost-efficient manner

   A) I only
   B) III only
   C) both I and II
   D) both II and III

18. Which of the following is a key feature of real-business-cycle models?

   I. calibration techniques
   II. deductive analysis
   III. technology shocks

   A) I only
   B) II only
   C) both I and III
   D) both II and III

19. Quantitative theory is

   A) the use of numerical calculations to develop theoretical models that fit observed business-cycle facts.
   B) the use of models of heterogeneous agents to explain how coordination failures can induce cycles.
   C) a highly deductive approach that emphasizes the development of very simple models.
   D) a highly deductive approach that emphasizes the development of abstract models.

20. In contrast to macroeconomists who use standard approaches to developing models, those who use a quantitative-theory approach to macroeconomic theory conclude that their models are successful if

   A) qualitative predictions about the effects of macroeconomic policy actions correspond to those we observe in the real world.
   B) real-world observations of macroeconomic variables square with their model's deductively generated predictions.
   C) data generated artificially by the models exhibit business cycles that nearly match those in actual economies.
   D) qualitative predictions of their theories receive statistical support from real-world observations.

Short-Answer Questions

1. What are time series data?

2. What is price inertia?

3. What is a market failure?

4. In general, what is an economic externality?

5. What is a macroeconomic externality?

6. What is the administered pricing hypothesis?

7. In new Keynesian models, what is a coordination failure?

8. What is a strategic interaction?

9. What is outside money?

10. What is a technique in which real-business-cycle theorists imbed estimated elasticities and initial data into their theoretical models in an effort to determine if their models generate cyclical movements in macroeconomic variables that mimic those of real-world economies?

Chapter 14: What Should Policymakers Do? — Objectives and Targets of Macroeconomic Policy

Chapter Summary

Most macroeconomists focus on three sets of goals that monetary and fiscal policymakers might contemplate pursuing: low and stable inflation, high and stable real output, and high and stable employment. Two laws commit U.S. macroeconomic policymakers to these goals. One is the Employment Act of 1946, which requires all federal government agencies to seek to attain the objectives of "maximum employment, production, and purchasing power." The other is the 1978 Full Employment and Balanced Growth Act, or Humphrey-Hawkins Act, which set an unemployment rate goal of 3 percent and an inflation goal of 0 percent.

The U.S. Federal Reserve System (the "Fed") is partly private, partly public institution that Congress intentionally did not call a "central bank" when it established the Fed in 1913. A fundamental objective in the establishment of the Fed was the prevention of banking panics, but after the Fed failed to halt widespread banking panics following the stock market crash of 1929, in 1935 Congress centralized power over the Fed within the Board of Governors of the Federal Reserve System. The seven members of the Board of Governors set the Fed's discount rate, which is the interest rate that the twelve Federal Reserve banks charge on loans that they make to U.S. banking institutions. The Board of Governors also determine reserve requirements, or rules under which banks must set aside a fraction of each dollar of checking deposits in a cash reserve, either in the banks' vaults or in the form of deposits at Federal Reserve banks, and it has oversight authority over the Federal Reserve banks. Finally, the Board governors serve on the Federal Reserve's 12-member Federal Open Market Committee (FOMC), which also includes five voting members who are presidents of Federal Reserve banks. The FOMC determines policy for the Fed's open-market operations, which are the Fed's purchases and sales of U.S. government securities.

Open-market operations are the primary means by which the Fed influences the amount of money in circulation in the United States. In the simplest banking system, if q is the required reserve ratio for transaction (checking) deposits that constitute the bulk of the nominal money stock, then a change in deposits is equal to $\Delta D = (1/q) \times \Delta R$, where ΔR denotes a change in bank reserves induced by an open-market operation. Because q is a fraction, $1/q$ is a number greater than one, so an open-market purchase or sale has causes a multiple change in the amount of transaction deposits included in the total stock of money. Thus, the ratio $1/q$ is a "money multiplier." The overall money multiplier realistically is smaller than this ratio, because people hold some money in the form of currency and banks typically hold excess reserves, thereby reducing the amount of reserves available to lend in the process of multiple deposit expansion.

Most central banks, including the Fed, typically have sought to achieve intermediate targets, or target values for a macroeconomic variable whose value a central bank tries to control because it feels that doing so is consistent with its ultimate objectives. There are two rationales for using an intermediate target in monetary policy. One is the difficulty that central bank officials have understanding and reaching agreement about the ways in which monetary policy affects inflation, real output, and employment in the short and long run. The other is that even if central bank policymakers could unanimously conclude that they know how their policy actions influence economic activity, they typically possess limited information about the economy.

Information about potential intermediate target variables may be more readily available, as compared with information about ultimate objectives. Consequently, by aiming to achieve an intermediate target, a central bank can more infer in a more timely manner whether or not it may be on the way to achieving the basic intent of its policies. A useful intermediate target variable should exhibit four key attributes. First, it should be frequently observable. Second, achieving a target value for an intermediate variable should be consistent with achieving the central bank's ultimate objectives. Third, defining and measuring an intermediate target variable should be a straightforward task. Finally, an intermediate target variable should be a macroeconomic variable whose value the central bank can readily influence.

There are several types of macroeconomic variables that might be considered as intermediate monetary policy targets. One set of potential intermediate target variables are monetary aggregates, or alternative measures of the nominal money stock, which various macroeconomic theories indicate should influence aggregate demand, and, thus, price level and, possibly, real output and employment. One problem with monetary targets is that regulatory and technological changes have blurred the lines among various financial assets that function as money. Another problem is a breakdown in the previously consistent relationship between the basic M1 and M2 aggregates and GDP that occurred in the 1980s and 1990s. Another set of possible intermediate target variables are credit aggregates, or measures of the volume of lending, although these pose problems similar to those entailed in using monetary aggregates for intermediate targeting. A third potential intermediate monetary policy target is a nominal interest rate, which central banks can observe daily and often by the minute and which central bank policy actions definitely influence. Problems entailed in using a nominal interest rate as an intermediate target variable is that interest rates and economic activity are not always closely related, and central banks must choose from a number of different interest rates on financial instruments with short and long maturities.

Nominal GDP is yet another possible intermediate target variable. Though nominal GDP data are not available more frequently than observations of real GDP and the price level, by definition nominal GDP equals real GDP times the GDP price deflator, and so minimizing variations in nominal GDP output would tend to contain volatility in either of these ultimate goal variables. For example, Figure 14 shows how targeting nominal GDP would automatically offset inflation in the face of a rise in aggregate demand. An increase in aggregate demand would cause a movement from point A to point B, which would tend to increase both the price level and real output in the short run, thereby causing nominal income to rise above the target level Y^*. Maintaining the nominal income target would require a policy action that would push aggregate demand back downward, thereby automatically eliminating the potential for short- or long-run increases in the price level.

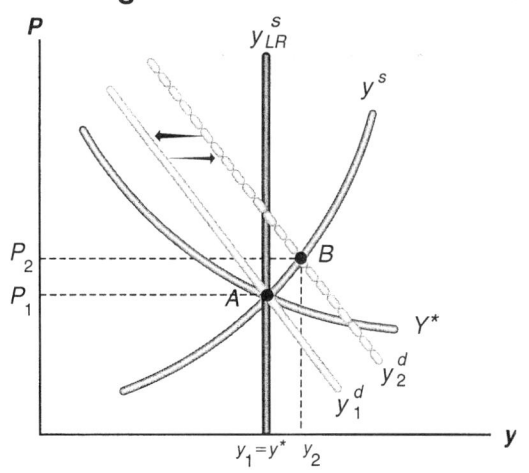

Figure 14: Limiting Inflation with a Nominal GDP Target

Application of the *IS-LM* model indicates that adopting a nominal interest target makes aggregate demand more stable when money demand is highly volatile while aggregate desired expenditures are relatively stable. By way of contrast, using a monetary aggregate as an intermediate target stabilizes aggregate demand when aggregate desired expenditures are variable while money demand is relatively stable. Application of the theory of aggregate demand and aggregate supply indicates that nominal GDP targeting would automatically stabilize aggregate demand and would limit the inflationary effects of variations in aggregate supply. This has led a number of economists to suggest that the Fed should target nominal GDP.

A government budget deficit occurs whenever the government spends more than it receives in taxes and other sources of revenue. To finance deficits, the U.S. government must borrow by issuing Treasury bills, notes, and bonds. By so doing, the government accumulates an indebtedness to those who purchase such securities. The accumulated amount of all outstanding amounts owed to private holders of government-issued securities is the net national debt, and so each year that the government runs a deficit adds to the national debt. There are two social burdens that can stem from accumulating a large national debt. One is that debts accumulated in current years must be repaid in the future, which requires future generations to give up spending power that they otherwise could retain if they did not have to repaying debts owing to current government deficits. The other is that a portion of national debt repayments entail flows of U.S. resources to citizens of other nations who hold domestic government debt.

A fundamental problem faced by governments and central banks is that domestic and international objectives sometimes conflict. As a result, governments and central banks often must determine which of these goals they should seek to achieve. Determining which policymakers should take responsibility for achieving the internal-balance or external-balance objectives is the assignment problem in policymaking. The incorrect assignment of these objectives between a central bank and a government fiscal authority can lead to greater departures from external and internal balance goals. To achieve a correct assignment of objectives that can permit both policymakers to achieve these goals simultaneously, the policymakers must take into account the extent to which capital is mobile and whether the exchange rate is fixed or flexible.

Key Terms and Concepts

Assignment problem
Discount rate
Federal Open Market Committee (FOMC)
Intermediate target
Mercantilism
Monetary aggregates
National debt
Open-market operations
Reserve requirements
Ultimate goals

Multiple-Choice Questions

1. Which of the following is a goal of Federal Reserve monetary policy?

    I. attaining low and stable inflation rates
    II. attaining an equitable income distribution
    III. attaining high and stable unemployment rates

    A) I only
    B) II only
    C) both I and III
    D) both II and III

2. Which of the following responses to inflation does not entail a redistribution of resources?

    A) the shifting of wealth from a mortgage lender to a homeowner.
    B) the expense of resources by a business to economize on its money holdings
    C) the transfer of income from taxpayers to the government in a nonindexed tax system.
    D) the reduction in real interest payments that a business must make on its outstanding debt to a bank

3. Which of the following inflation costs results primarily from variability in inflation rather than from inflation per se?

    I. reductions in investment and capital accumulation
    II. slowed pace of introducing new products
    III. the costs of changing prices

    A) both I and II
    B) both II and III
    C) both I and III
    D) I, II, and III

4. The Federal Reserve's targets and overall strategies for its open-market operations are determined by which one of the following, without input from any other individuals?

    A) the Board of Governors of the Federal Reserve System
    B) the President of the Federal Reserve Bank of New York
    C) the twelve Federal Reserve bank presidents
    D) the Federal Open Market Committee

5. The primary means by which the Federal Reserve influences the total amount of money in circulation is through

   A) changes in the required reserve ratio.
   B) foreign exchange market operations.
   C) changes in the discount rate.
   D) open-market operations.

6. Which of the following is an important characteristic of an intermediate monetary policy target?

   I. frequent observability
   II. easily defined and measured
   III. consistent with ultimate goals

   A) I and II only
   B) II and III only
   C) I and III only
   D) I, II, and III

7. What is the term for an economic variable that the Federal Reserve tries to control in an effort to achieve its ultimate goals?

   A) an intermediate target
   B) an proximate policy tool
   C) an intermediate instrument
   D) a proximate policy instrument

8. If the Federal Reserve's goal were to choose an intermediate target variable that is most frequently observable, then its choice would be

   A) a monetary aggregate.
   B) a credit aggregate.
   C) an interest rate.
   D) nominal GDP.

9. Which of the following would tend to make an interest rate a preferable intermediate target variable, as compared solely with targeting a monetary aggregate?

   I. sizable volatility of the demand for real money balances
   II. significant variability of real government expenditures
   III. significant volatility of autonomous investment expenditures

   A) I only
   B) III only
   C) both I and II
   D) both II and III

10. Which of the following would tend to make a monetary aggregate a preferable intermediate target variable, as compared solely with targeting an interest rate?

    I. significant variability of autonomous real saving
    II. significant variability of autonomous real exports
    III. sizable volatility of the demand for real money balances

    A) I only
    B) III only
    C) both I and II
    D) both II and III

11. According to the supply-side perspective on fiscal policymaking, reducing the effective tax rate on saving would

    I. increase the supply of loanable funds.
    II. reduce equilibrium investment in new capital goods.
    III. cause the aggregate production function to rotate downward in the future.

    A) I only
    B) III only
    C) both I and II
    D) both II and III

12. According to the supply-side perspective on fiscal policymaking, reducing the effective tax rate on investment would

    I. reduce the demand for loanable funds.
    II. raise equilibrium investment in new capital goods.
    III. cause the aggregate production function to rotate upward in the future.

    A) I only
    B) III only
    C) both I and II
    D) both II and III

13. The supply-side perspective on the effects of fiscal policies implies that a higher marginal income tax rate

    A) causes the supply of labor to increase.
    B) causes the demand for labor to increase.
    C) generates a leftward movement along the aggregate production function.
    D) generates a rightward movement along the aggregate production function.

14. Which of the following is true of the U.S. net national debt?

    A) The net national debt entails a burden for the current generation but has no consequences for future generations.
    B) As a percentage of gross domestic product, the net national debt has increased considerably since the mid-1990s.
    C) The portion of the net national debt held by residents of other nations has increased since the mid-1990s.
    D) The net national debt generates net income for the U.S. Treasury in the form of interest payments from abroad.

15. A social burden of the U.S. net national debt is

    A) transfers from residents of nations who are net lenders to the U.S. government to residents of nations who are net borrowers from the U.S. government.
    B) transfers from U.S. residents whose taxes fund interest payments to residents of other nations who hold debts issued by the U.S. government.
    C) the implied decrease in fiscal budget surpluses generated by increases in the size of the net national debt.
    D) the implied increase in fiscal budget deficits generated by reductions in the size of the net national debt.

16. According to the supply-side perspective on fiscal policymaking, a larger government budget surplus

   A) can result in higher real income growth, because a larger budget surplus boosts the real interest rate.
   B) can result in lower real income growth, because a larger budget surplus crowds out private investment.
   C) can contribute to lower real income growth if the government allocates the available funds to unproductive uses.
   D) can contribute to higher real income growth if the surplus results from a reduction in government spending without accompanying tax changes.

17. According to the supply-side perspective on fiscal policymaking, larger government budget deficit

   A) can result in higher real income growth, because a larger budget deficit boosts the real interest rate.
   B) can result in lower real income growth, because a larger budget deficit crowds out private investment.
   C) can contribute to higher real income growth if the government spends funds less efficiently than private households and businesses.
   D) can contribute to lower real income growth if the deficit results from a reduction in taxes without accompanying changes in government spending.

18. Which of the following goals are at issue in the policy assignment problem?

   A) internal balance and external balance
   B) internal balance and government budget balance
   C) external balance and government budget balance
   D) private payments balance and government budget balance

19. If the exchange rate is fixed, real income is below its target value, and there is a private payments deficit, then the appropriate assignment of policy objectives with very high capital mobility is

   A) assignment of private payments balance to the government and external balance to the central bank.
   B) assignment of government budget balance to the government and internal balance to the central bank.
   C) assignment of internal balance to the government and external balance to the central bank.
   D) assignment of external balance to the government and internal balance to the central bank.

20. Which of the following is a rationale for using nominal GDP as an intermediate target variable instead of either a monetary aggregate or an interest rate?

   I. Nominal GDP targeting stabilizes real GDP and the price level completely in the face of variations in aggregate supply.
   II. Nominal GDP targeting automatically offsets the effects of aggregate demand variations on real GDP and the price level.
   III. Nominal GDP can be observed with greater frequency.

   A) I only
   B) II only
   C) both I and III
   D) both II and III

Short-Answer Questions

1. What federal legislation requires the Federal Reserve to justify its monetary policies to Congress?

2. What are the explicit inflation and unemployment rate goals of the Humphrey-Hawkins Act of 1978?

3. What federal legislation requires the government to pursue the goals of maximum employment, maximum output production, and maximum purchasing power of money?

4. What is the discount rate?

5. What are open-market operations?

6. What is an intermediate target?

7. What is the net national debt?

8. According to the supply-side policy perspective, how can larger government budget deficits reduce the rate of economic growth?

9. According to the supply-side policy perspective, how can larger government budget surpluses contribute to lower economic growth?

10. What is the assignment problem in macroeconomic policymaking?

Chapter 15: What Can Policymakers Accomplish? — Rules versus Discretion in Macroeconomic Policy

Chapter Summary

Policy time lags are intervals between the need for a policy action and the ultimate effects of that action on an economic variable. There are three types of time lags in macroeconomic policymaking. The first of these, the recognition lag, is the time between the need for a macroeconomic policy action and the recognition of that need. The second policy time lag is the response lag, which is the time between recognition of the need for a change in macroeconomic policy and the actual implementation of that change. Finally, the transmission lag is the time that passes before an implemented policy fully exerts its macroeconomic effects. Policy time lags can make pursuing a successful countercyclical problematical, because policy actions actually may add to cyclical fluctuations in real income via well-meaning but ill-timed attempts to stabilize real income. Hence, discretionary policymaking, or macroeconomic policy responses made on an ad hoc basis, could end up destabilizing the economy. In the presence of time lags, it is possible that a policy rule under which a central bank or government binds or commits by following a policy strategy no matter what events might take place, could lead to greater macroeconomic stability.

Proponents of discretionary policies admit that policy time lags can pose serious problems but argue that central banks and governments are uniquely positioned to succeed in such endeavors more often than they might fail. They contend that situations can arise in which macroeconomic policymakers may have more complete information about the economy, as compared with the knowledge possessed by households and firms and that these policymakers face fewer constraints in their responses to new information about changing market conditions. Indeed, the public interest theory of macroeconomic policymaking views policymakers as altruistic individuals who seek the best outcomes for society as a whole. In contrast, adherents of the public choice theory of policymaking view central banks and governments as institutions that pursue their own self interest.

Theories of discretionary policymaking and inflation indicate that central bank credibility is important for maintaining low inflation. The reasoning behind this conclusion is illustrated in Figure 15, in which the current equilibrium real output level is y_1 but the nation's central bank desires for real output to rise toward the economy's capacity output level y^* while limiting the amount of the increase in the price level that would result from the increase in aggregate demand that would be required. If workers know that the central bank has this incentive to raise aggregate demand, then they will seek higher wages. This would raise business costs, thereby causing aggregate supply to shift leftward and reducing the production of real output. The result is no net change in equilibrium real output and in increase in the price level. Because of the time inconsistency problem, in which policymaker commitment is inconsistent with the strategies of workers and firms if the policymaker can alter his or her policy strategy at a later time, the only way that central banks can prevent such an inflation bias from occurring is by following through on believable commitments not to raise aggregate demand. Only central banks whose policies are credible can make such believable commitments.

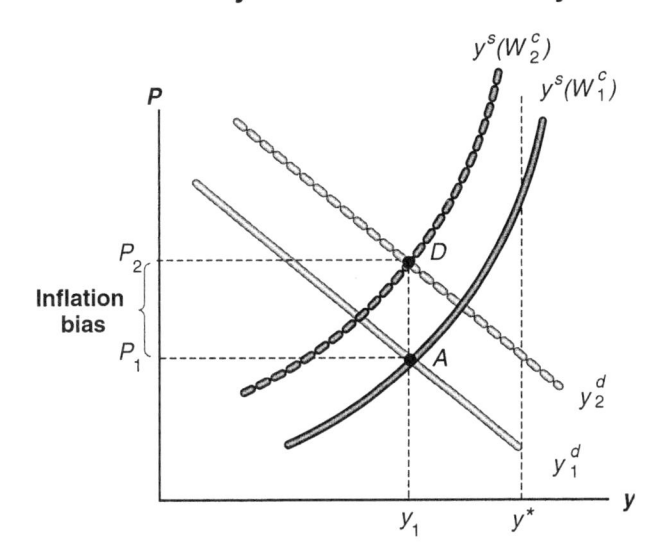

Figure 15: The Inflationary Bias of Discretionary Monetary Policy

Monetary policy credibility would be enhanced if wages were completely indexed, eliminating the trade-off between inflation and real output, but full indexation makes real output more variable in the face of supply shocks. A possible way to try to constrain inflation directly would be to amend national constitutions to make inflation above certain levels illegal. Central banks typically attempt to establish credibility by developing reputations for commitments to low inflation. Their reputations can be bolstered by appointments of central bankers who are known to dislike inflation. Another possible approach would be to establish contracts with central bankers that punish them for bad inflation performance and reward them for achieving low inflation.

Recent studies have shown that countries with more independent central banks also have lower average inflation rates and less inflation variability. Consequently, a number of economists have proposed increasing the autonomy of central bankers without necessarily reducing their accountability. Some have proposed reforming the Fed by increasing its autonomy while making it more accountable for its actions. Such reforms, they contend, would increase the Fed's credibility to low inflation, thereby leading to actual inflation reductions.

There are three ways in which fiscal policymakers potentially could gain greater credibility in an effort to overcome the time inconsistency problem that they also face. One might be to develop hard and fast rules for how a legislature can tax and spend, perhaps by establishing special requirements for any tax and spending bills that a representative introduces, such as requiring the representative to propose how the bill could be adopted while keeping the government's budget in balance. Another approach might be to establish bipartisan commissions charged with examining controversial spending or tax plans and with making specific recommendations for fiscal actions that the legislature preauthorizes the commission to undertake. A third, more direct approach might be to amend a nation's constitution to make unbalanced budgets illegal.

Exchange rate devaluations, which are policy-induced reductions in the value of a nation's currency in terms of the currencies of other nations, reduce the expense that foreign residents must incur to obtain a nation's currency and buy its goods. This can cause the nation's exports to expand, thereby raising aggregate demand and causing a short-term rise in real output. Hence, nations have faced a time inconsistency problem in their exchange rate policies, in that there is always an incentive for a nation with an open economy to devalue its currency to push real output toward its capacity level, even though such devaluations often are associated with upticks in the inflation rate. Consequently, discretionary exchange rate policy can lead to an inflationary bias. Attempting to fix the exchange rate requires establishing and maintaining credibility to a nation's exchange-rate commitment. In the nineteenth century, many nations used a gold standard, in which the values of their currencies were tied to the value of gold, as a means of establishing more credible linkages among their exchange rates. In today's fiat money system, all that stands behind national currency values is the credibility of nations' monetary and exchange-rate policies. Therefore, nations with fixed exchange rates must persuade those who hold their currencies, that the official exchange rate is consistent with the underlying terms at which their nations trade goods with other countries, and these nations must have sufficient reserves of other nations' currencies available for use in purchasing their own nation's currency when doing so is necessary to maintain the fixed exchange rate. If currency traders anticipate any devaluations, they will sell the nation's currency and depress its value, requiring the nation's central bank to purchase the nation's currency with other nations' currencies that it has on hand. If the nation's foreign currency reserves fall to levels that are too low to maintain an official exchange rate, then the nation's commitment to the officially announced exchange rate will not be credible, and the nation will forced to devalue.

Because of the difficulties inherent in fixing the exchange rate, some nations have attempted to cooperate in maintaining fixed exchange rates. From shortly after the end of World War II until 1971, an international coordination effort called the Bretton Woods system set and maintained fixed exchange rates relative to the value of the U.S. dollar, which in turn was linked to the value of gold. The dollar's link to gold ended in 1971, and several nations decided to allow their exchange rates to float freely in the foreign exchange markets. The European Community (EC) of nations, after several failed attempts to fix exchange rates during the 1970s, established the European Monetary System (EMS) for maintaining fixed rates of exchange among their currencies in 1979. This system required EC central banks to intervene in foreign exchange markets whenever their exchange rates varied more than specified percentages from agreed rates of exchange. In 1992, however, the EMS experienced a major credibility breakdown, but current members of the European Union (EU) formally remain committed to adopting a single currency, called the "Euro," by the beginning of the 21st century.

Some nations, such as Hong Kong, Singapore, and Argentina, had adopted a currency board approach, in which their monetary policymaker is a currency board that issues local currency that is 100 percent backed by the currency of another nation. Proponents of currency boards contend that this approach to a fixed exchange rate is more credible than the standard approach because the 100 percent backing constraint ensures that a government cannot issue more currency than the amount of foreign exchange reserves it has on hand.

Key Terms and Concepts

Capacity output
Central banker contract
Conservative central banker
Currency board
Devaluation
Discretionary policymaking
Inflation bias
Policy credibility
Policy rule
Policy time lags
Public choice theory
Public interest theory
Recognition lag
Response lag
Time inconsistency problem
Transmission lag

Multiple-Choice Questions

1. What type of monetary policy does the Federal Reserve conduct if its policy actions add to upward and downward fluctuations in economic activity?

    A) a countercyclical monetary policy
    B) an unsystematic monetary policy
    C) a systematic monetary policy
    D) a procyclical monetary policy

2. What is the term for a central banker who dislikes inflation more than others in society?

    A) a liberal central banker
    B) an inflationary central banker
    C) a conservative central banker
    D) an contractionary central banker

3. What type of monetary policy does the Fed conduct if it manages to offset upward and downward movements in economic activity?

    A) a countercyclical monetary policy
    B) an unsystematic monetary policy
    C) a systematic monetary policy
    D) a procyclical monetary policy

4. What is the term for a Federal Reserve precommitment to following a specific monetary policy strategy without regard to economic conditions that may emerge?

    A) a discretionary policy stance
    B) a monetary policy strategy
    C) a tactical policy stance
    D) a monetary policy rule

5. Suppose that there is a sudden rise in aggregate demand. If it takes three weeks for the Federal Reserve to realize that the increase in aggregate demand has occurred, then what is this time interval?

    A) the response lag
    B) the recognition lag
    C) the intermediate lag
    D) the transmission lag

6. Suppose that the Federal Reserve determines that, on average, it takes 49 weeks for any policy action that it may take to have its final effects on economic activity. What is this period called?

   A) the response lag
   B) the recognition lag
   C) the intermediate lag
   D) the transmission lag

7. About a week after an Federal Open Market Committee (FOMC) meeting, there is a sudden decline in aggregate demand that causes real output to begin to decline. Shortly thereafter, Fed officials realize that there is a need for a policy action, and six weeks after that, at the next FOMC meeting, the Fed decides to try to expand aggregate demand to its original level. What is the term for the four-week interval before the second FOMC meeting?

   A) the response lag
   B) the recognition lag
   C) the intermediate lag
   D) the transmission lag

8. Suppose that the Federal Reserve decides to try to keep the price level from rising as a result of a recent increase in consumer spending. By the time that the Federal Reserve implements a policy to address this problem, however, consumer spending and aggregate prices have returned to their former levels. This is an example of

   A) procyclical monetary policy.
   B) countercyclical monetary policy.
   C) maintaining a monetary policy rule.
   D) honoring a monetary policy commitment.

9. Suppose that there is a sudden rise in investment spending by businesses that raises aggregate demand and begins to cause a short-run increase in the price level. The Federal Reserve quickly reduces the quantity of money to stabilize aggregate demand and the price level. This would be an example of

   A) procyclical monetary policy.
   B) countercyclical monetary policy.
   C) maintaining a monetary policy rule.
   D) honoring a monetary policy commitment.

10. According to recent theory, one possible explanation for an inflationary bias of monetary policy could be

   A) an unwillingness of a central bank to pursue discretionary monetary policies.
   B) a government's decision to appoint of a conservative central banker.
   C) the inability of a central bank to credibly precommit its policies.
   D) a central bank's commitment to a monetary policy rule.

11. A politically independent central bank is one

   A) whose budget cannot be influenced by governmental actions.
   B) whose balance sheet cannot be influenced by governmental actions.
   C) that is insulated from governmental control over its internal decision-making process for monetary policy.
   D) that is insulated from governmental control over its choice of whether or not to hold government securities.

12. An economically independent central bank is one

   A) that has the ability to make policy choices without governmental interference.
   B) that has the ability to control its own budget without governmental interference.
   C) whose policymaking board can vote to adopt discretionary monetary policy actions.
   D) whose policymaking board can commit itself to policy rules without fear of governmental reprisals.

13. Which of the following does recent evidence indicate is a result of greater central bank independence?

   I. reduced output variability
   II. lower average inflation
   III. lower inflation volatility

   A) both I and II
   B) both I and III
   C) both II and III
   D) I, II, and III

14. The commitment to monetary policy strategy aimed at a clear policy goal is

   A) an intermediate targeting procedure that may be changed as conditions warrant.
   B) a proximate targeting strategy that may be altered as conditions warrant.
   C) discretionary monetary policy.
   D) a monetary policy rule.

15. Which of the following is a common rationale for discretionary fiscal policymaking in the United States?

    I. a potential informational advantage that the government may have in compiling and processing information
    II. the possibility that the government, unlike private individuals, may unconstrained by self-interest
    III. shorter time lags, as compared with those that the Federal Reserve experiences

    A) both I and II only
    B) both I and III only
    C) both II and III only
    D) I, II, and III

16. According to the public choice theory of macroeconomic policymaking,

    A) policymakers pursue the welfare of society as a whole.
    B) policymakers pursue their own interests and objectives.
    C) governments and central banks have inherent informational advantages over private individuals.
    D) government and central banks face fewer constraints in their ability to react to unexpected events.

17. According to the theory of discretionary policymaking, which of the following results from a lack of policy credibility?

    I. higher inflation
    II. lower real output
    III. higher unemployment

    A) I only
    B) both I and III only
    C) both II and III only
    D) I, II, and III

18. A policy-induced reduction in the value of a nation's currency relative to other currencies is called

    A) depreciation.
    B) appreciation.
    C) devaluation.
    D) revaluation.

19. In the context of exchange-rate policy, the term credibility refers to

    A) the believability of foreign exchange market speculators' intentions to profit from anticipated exchange rate changes.
    B) the believability of a commitment by a nation's policymakers to a stated intention to keep the exchange rate fixed.
    C) the likelihood that a nation's central bank will increase the amount of money in circulation in the face of a currency depreciation.
    D) the likelihood that a nation's central bank will decrease the amount of money in circulation in the face of a currency appreciation.

20. The rate at which a good produced in one nation may be exchanged for a good produced in another nation is called the

    A) nominal exchange rate.
    B) nominal interest rate.
    C) real exchange rate.
    D) real interest rate.

Short-Answer Questions

1. What is the time between the need for a macroeconomic action and a policymaker's realization of the need?

2. What is the time between a macroeconomic policymaker's realization that there is a need for a policy action and its actual implementation of such an action?

3. What is the time between a macroeconomic policymaker's implementation of a policy action and the action's ultimate effect on economic variables such as prices, employment, and output?

4. About how long is the transmission lag of monetary policy in the United States?

5. What type of policy does a macroeconomic policymaker conduct when it departs from a preannounced policy strategy because of changes in economic conditions?

6. What is an economy's capacity output level?

7. What is the key element of the public interest theory of macroeconomic policymaking?

8. What is the key element of the public choice theory of macroeconomic policymaking?

9. With what type of monetary policy arrangement has New Zealand experimented?

10. What is a currency board?

Chapter 16: Policymaking in the World Economy — International Dimensions of Macroeconomic Policy

Chapter Summary

Foreign exchange risk is the possibility that variations in market values of assets can take place as a result of changes in the value of a nation's currency. There are three fundamental types of foreign exchange risk. One is accounting risk, which is the risk that a country's residents may variations in the market value of their foreign asset holdings solely because of changes in home-currency valuations resulting from exchange-rate variations. Another is transaction risk, which is the possibility that the value of a financial asset relating to the funding of a foreign-currency-denominated transaction could change because an exchange rate movement could affect the underlying value of the transaction. The third type of foreign exchange risk is currency risk, or the possibility of variations in underlying asset returns due to exchange rate volatility. Individuals, firms, and governments can hedge against such risks, or adopt strategies intended to offset the risk arising from exchange rate variations, by trading forward currency contracts, interest rate forward contracts, currency swaps, or interest rate swaps. Nevertheless, hedging is a costly activity, which provides one possible justification for fixed exchange rates as a way to reduce or even eliminate hedging costs.

According to the theory of optimal currency areas, however, exchange-rate flexibility is desirable if labor and other productive factors cannot move freely across national or regional boundaries. If productive factors are immobile between different nations or geographic regions, then the exchange rate absorbs the burden of adjustment to changing relative demand and supply conditions. Exchange-rate adjustments help speed the relief from pressures of rising unemployment that can arise from changes in the relative demands for the regions' products. This theory indicates that a fixed exchange rate is clearly desirable only for nations or regions in which labor and other factors of production can move at minimal cost across national borders or regional boundaries. Then the nations or regions would constitute an optimal currency area, which is a geographic region within which fixed exchange rates can be maintained without hindering international adjustment.

Greater interrelationships among markets for goods, services, factors of production, and financial assets, or international economic integration, facilitates international arbitrage, or the act of buying a good in one nation for profitable sale in another. This makes the attainment of purchasing power parity and interest rate parity conditions more likely. Eurocurrency markets, which are markets for funds denominated in currencies issued by nations beyond the borders of a nation in which the funds actually are held, have contributed to greater capital mobility. At the extreme eventuality of perfect capital mobility, financial resources would be as mobile across nations' borders as they are within nations' borders.

The *BP* schedule is perfectly elastic under perfect capital mobility, because in this situation the slightest change in the nation's interest rate would cause very large movements of funds across its borders. Monetary policy cannot influence aggregate demand under fixed exchange rates and perfect capital mobility, while fiscal policy has its largest possible effect on aggregate demand in this setting. In contrast, fiscal policy cannot affect aggregate demand with floating exchange rates and perfect capital mobility, while monetary policy has its greatest influence on aggregate demand in this environment. This latter conclusion is illustrated in Figure 16. In panel (a), a reduction in the quantity of money causes the *LM* schedule to shift to the left. This results in a private payments surplus at point *B*, which causes the nation's currency to appreciate. As a result, imports decline and exports rise, thereby causing autonomous aggregate expenditures to fall and generating a leftward shift in the *IS* schedule. Consequently, equilibrium real income falls by the largest possible amount, to y_3 at point *C*. In panel (b), a reduction in real government spending initially causes the *IS* schedule to shift to the left, which leads to a private payments deficit at point *B*. As a result, the nation's currency depreciates, which induces a rise in imports and a decline in exports, so that the *IS* schedule shifts back to the right. On net, therefore, equilibrium real income remains unaffected by the reduction in government expenditures.

Figure 16: The Effects of Monetary and Fiscal Policy Contractions with Perfect Capital Mobility and Floating Exchange Rates

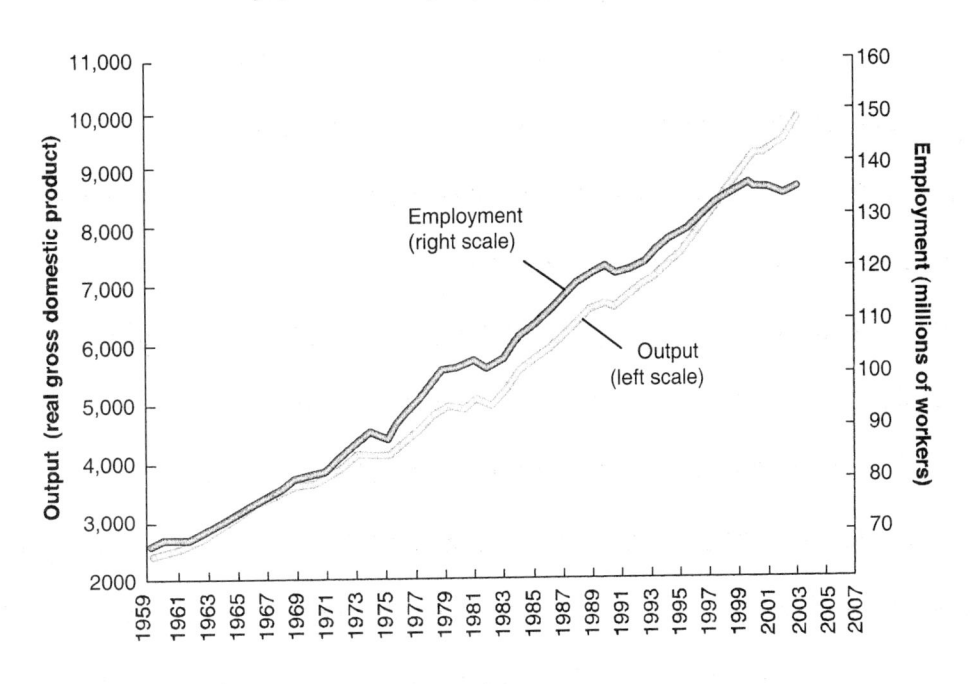

Greater international economic integration affects the growth prospects and policies of the world's nations. With significant capital mobility, financial resources flow across national borders in pursuit of the highest possible rates of return, and many of the locales that offer the highest returns. Increased capital mobility can thereby contribute to a higher rate of global per capita income growth by efficiently directing capital resources. At the same time, however, the capability of investors to move financial resources across national borders exposes countries to greater risks of experiencing international financial crises. According to one view, international financial crises arise from a mismatch between the exchange value of a nation's currency with the value implied by such economic fundamentals as the nation's overall economic performance and monetary and fiscal policies. A second perspective suggests that if traders develop a perception that policymakers' commitments to current exchange rates are not credible, then self-fulfilling anticipations can lead to sizable movements in currency values that help set off a crisis. A third view emphasizes the role of government policies that create moral hazard problems that can induce borrowers to misallocate funds they obtain from lenders.

The International Monetary Fund (IMF) and the World Bank are multinational institutions at the focus of present world effort to prevent and stem international financial crises. The IMF is funded by quota subscriptions of member nations, and it establishes conditionality requirements limiting the uses to which national governments can make of funds they borrow from the IMF. Although both the World Bank and the IMF are interested in promoting global economic growth, this is more fundamentally the World Bank's objective that it seeks to attain via its programs providing longer-term credit to developing countries. The IMF is more directly involved in providing loans intended to stabilize international financial markets and to promote stable exchange rate arrangements.

In recent years multinational policymakers have sought to do a better job of anticipating international financial crises in advance, so that they can better offset their effects or perhaps even prevent crises from taking place. Toward this end, they have tried to identify economic variables that might serve as financial crisis indicators within an early warning system, or mechanism for monitory financial and economic data for signals of problems that might bring about a crisis situation. Many critics, however, contend that the policies of the institutions themselves can contribute to the potential for international financial crises, and they have offered a number of alternative proposals for how multinational policymaking institutions might be reformed.

Key Terms and Concepts

Accounting risk
Conditionality
Currency risk
Dollarization
Early warning system
Economic fundamentals
Eurocurrency markets
Ex ante conditionality
Ex post conditionality
Foreign exchange risk
Financial crisis
Financial crisis indicator
Foreign direct investment
Hedge
International economic integration
International Monetary Fund
Optimal currency area
Perfect capital mobility
Portfolio investment
Quota subscription
Speculative attack
Transaction risk
World Bank

Multiple-Choice Questions

1. The risk that changes in exchange rates can affect the valuations of businesses assets and liabilities and thereby influence their net worth even if market rates of return are unaffected is called

   A) transaction risk.
   B) accounting risk.
   C) financial risk.
   D) currency risk.

2. The risk that underlying rates of return on financial assets denominated in other currencies may vary as a result of unexpected changes in exchange rates is called

   A) transaction risk.
   B) accounting risk.
   C) financial risk.
   D) currency risk.

3. Which of the following would improve the likelihood that two geographic regions might constitute an optimal currency area?

   I.   a common language
   II. few natural barriers to migration
   III. legal barriers to employment of foreign residents

   A) I only
   B) III only
   C) both I and II
   D) both II and III

4. Which of the following is a rationale for a system of fixed exchange rates?

   I.   strengthening the aggregate demand effects of home monetary policy when capital is perfectly mobile across national borders
   II. providing a shock-absorber mechanism when labor is immobile across national borders
   III. saving a nation's residents the costs of hedging against foreign exchange risks

   A) I only
   B) III only
   C) both I and II
   D) both II and III

5. Monetary policy has no effect on aggregate demand if there is

   A) perfect capital mobility and the exchange rate is fixed.
   B) perfect capital mobility and the exchange rate floats.
   C) no capital mobility and the exchange rate is fixed.
   D) no capital mobility and the exchange rate floats.

6. Fiscal policy has no effect on aggregate demand if there is

   A) perfect capital mobility and the exchange rate is fixed.
   B) perfect capital mobility and the exchange rate floats.
   C) no capital mobility and the exchange rate is fixed.
   D) no capital mobility and the exchange rate floats.

7. If there is perfect capital mobility and exchange rates are determined solely by market forces, then

   A) an expansionary monetary policy action has its largest possible effect on aggregate demand.
   B) a contractionary monetary policy action has its smallest possible effect on aggregate demand.
   C) an expansionary fiscal policy action has its largest possible effect on aggregate demand.
   D) a contractionary fiscal policy action has its largest possible effect on aggregate demand.

8. Consider a nation with perfect capital mobility and floating exchange rates. Suppose that the nation initially has attained private payments balance. A contractionary fiscal policy action will result in which one of following chains of events?

   A) It will cause the nominal interest rate to decline, thereby inducing a capital inflow that will result in a private payments surplus, which in turn will cause a currency appreciation and a decline in export spending that will reattain private payments balance.
   B) It will cause the nominal interest rate to increase, thereby inducing a capital outflow that will result in a private payments deficit, which in turn will cause a currency depreciation and a rise in export spending that will reattain private payments balance.
   C) It will cause the nominal interest rate to decline, thereby inducing a capital outflow that will result in a private payments deficit, which in turn will cause a currency depreciation and a rise in export spending that will reattain private payments balance.
   D) It will cause the nominal interest rate to increase, thereby inducing a capital inflow that will result in a private payments surplus, which in turn will cause a currency appreciation and a fall in export spending that will reattain private payments balance.

9. If there is perfect capital mobility and exchange rates are fixed, then

   A) an expansionary monetary policy action has its largest possible effect on aggregate demand.
   B) a contractionary monetary policy action has its largest possible effect on aggregate demand.
   C) an expansionary fiscal policy action has its largest possible effect on aggregate demand.
   D) a contractionary fiscal policy action has its smallest possible effect on aggregate demand.

10. Consider a nation with perfect capital mobility and floating exchange rates. Suppose that the nation initially has attained private payments balance. A contractionary monetary policy action will result in which one of following chains of events?

   A) It will cause the nominal interest rate to decline, thereby inducing a capital inflow that will result in a private payments surplus, which in turn will cause a currency appreciation and a decline in export spending that will reattain private payments balance.
   B) It will cause the nominal interest rate to increase, thereby inducing a capital outflow that will result in a private payments deficit, which in turn will cause a currency depreciation and a rise in export spending that will reattain private payments balance.
   C) It will cause the nominal interest rate to decline, thereby inducing a capital outflow that will result in a private payments deficit, which in turn will cause a currency depreciation and a rise in export spending that will reattain private payments balance.
   D) It will cause the nominal interest rate to increase, thereby inducing a capital inflow that will result in a private payments surplus, which in turn will cause a currency appreciation and a fall in export spending that will reattain private payments balance.

11. Consider a nation with perfect capital mobility and fixed exchange rates. Suppose that the nation initially has attained private payments balance. A contractionary monetary policy action will result in which one of following chains of events?

    A) It will cause the nominal interest rate to rise, thereby inducing a capital inflow and a private payments surplus, which in turn will induce the central bank to purchase foreign-currency-denominated assets that, with nonsterilized monetary policy, will cause the money stock to rise and push the interest rate back down.
    B) It will cause the nominal interest rate to decline, thereby inducing a capital outflow and a private payments deficit, which in turn will induce the central bank to sell foreign-currency-denominated assets that, with nonsterilized monetary policy, will cause the money stock to fall and push the interest rate down further.
    C) It will cause the nominal interest rate to decline, thereby inducing a capital inflow and a private payments surplus, which in turn will induce the central bank to sell foreign-currency-denominated assets that, with nonsterilized monetary policy, will cause the money stock to fall and push the interest rate down further.
    D) It will cause the nominal interest rate to rise, thereby inducing a capital inflow and a private payments surplus, which in turn will induce the central bank to sell foreign-currency-denominated assets that, with nonsterilized monetary policy, will cause the money stock to fall and push the interest rate further upward.

12. The main way that dollarization by other nations benefits the United States is

    A) the increased incentive that those nations thereby have to engage in trade with the United States.
    B) the greater influence that U.S. policymakers can thereby have on the economies of those nations.
    C) that foreign holdings of U.S. currency are backed by securities that generate interest income for the U.S. Treasury.
    D) that the greater dependence that those nations have on U.S. policymaking can give their governments political cover for their own policy weaknesses.

13. If a U.S. company purchases more than 10 percent of the ownership shares in a foreign enterprise, it engages in

    A) a speculative attack.
    B) portfolio investment.
    C) a quota subscription.
    D) foreign direct investment..

14. If a Canadian pension fund buys an amount of stock amounting to less than 10 percent of the total shares issued by an Indonesian firm, then it has engaged in

    A) a speculative attack.
    B) portfolio investment.
    C) a quota subscription.
    D) foreign direct investment.

15. The basic factors, such as an economy's underlying performance and its government's economic policies, which influence a nation's exchange rate are called

    A) economic fundamentals.
    B) financial crisis indicators.
    C) self-fulfilling anticipations.
    D) early warning system factors.

16. Increased global capital mobility

    I. contributes to world growth by allowing resources to flow to the most productive activities.
    II. provides international investors with greater capability to speedily shift funds from one nation to another.
    III. raises the potential for international financial crises that can detract from the economic stability of nations that are recipients of capital flows.

    A) I and II only
    B) I and III only
    C) II and II only
    D) I, II, and III

17. If a speculative attack on a nation's currency takes place simply because traders anticipate that it will be successful, then the reason for the attack is the existence of

    A) economic fundamentals.
    B) financial crisis indicators.
    C) self-fulfilling anticipations.
    D) early warning system factors.

18. A key difference between the objectives of the International Monetary Fund and the World Bank is that

    A) the International Monetary Fund is more interested in promoting long-term global economic growth.
    B) the World Bank is more heavily involved in developing financial crisis indicators for an early warning system.
    C) the World Bank is more interested in promoting short-term stability of international financial markets.
    D) the International Monetary Fund is more heavily involved in developing effective systems of international exchange rate arrangements.

19. When the International Monetary Fund places special conditions on receipts of loan installments after it has initially indicated that it will lend to a nation's government, it

    A) engages in a speculative attack.
    B) imposes ex ante conditionality.
    C) imposes ex post conditionality.
    D) has self-fulfilling anticipations.

20. The International Monetary Fund has developed financial crisis indicators in an effort to

    A) assist international investors in timing their speculative attacks.
    B) help foreign exchange traders determine when to sell currencies.
    C) provide early warning systems for use in preventing and containing crises.
    D) develop a measure of international stability for use in promoting global growth.

Short-Answer Questions

1. What is foreign exchange risk?

2. What is a hedge against foreign exchange risk?

3. What is an optimal currency area?

4. What is the term for an overall trend toward increased interactions and interrelationships among the world's markets for goods, services, and financial assets?

5. What is perfect capital mobility?

6. Why is the *BP* schedule horizontal when there is perfect capital mobility?

7. What is dollarization?

8. How does international portfolio investment differ from foreign direct investment?

9. What are the three different views on the underlying causes of international financial crises?

10. Why might multinational policymakers desire to develop an early warning system for international financial crises?

Answers to Questions

Chapter 1

Multiple-Choice Questions

1.	C	5.	D	9.	B	13.	B	17.	C
2.	C	6.	A	10.	A	14.	D	18.	D
3	A	7.	D	11.	C	15.	A	19.	B
4.	B	8.	D	12.	D	16.	C	20.	B

Short-Answer Questions

1. microeconomics

2. macroeconomics

3. microeconomic foundations

4. aggregation

5. domestic variables

6. international trade

7. the nation's standard of living

8. a merchandise trade surplus

9. below

10. above

Chapter 2

Multiple-Choice Questions

1. A
2. A
3. B
4. D
5. D
6. C
7. D
8. C
9. A
10. B
11. B
12. C
13. C
14. C
15. A
16. D
17. C
18. D
19. B
20. A

Short-Answer Questions

1. depreciation

2. a good that may be used to produce additional goods or services in the future

3. the current account

4. the official settlements balance

5. the net total of all private exchanges between a nation's residents and the rest of the world

6. zero

7. GDP price deflator = Nominal GDP / Real GDP.

8. the consumer price index, or the producer price index

9. chain-weight GDP

10. downward

Answers

Chapter 3

Multiple-Choice Questions

1. C
2. B
3. A
4. A
5. D
6. B
7. D
8. D
9. D
10. A
11. A
12. C
13. D
14. B
15. C
16. B
17. C
18. C
19. A
20. D

Short-Answer Questions

1. money illusion

2. the additional output produced by an additional unit of labor

3. Additional increases in employment eventually lead to smaller additional increases in output produced.

4. the classical aggregate supply schedule

5. the classical aggregate demand schedule

6. the equation of exchange

7. store of value

8. unit of account

9. standard of deferred payment

10. Cambridge equation

Chapter 4

Multiple-Choice Questions

1. A
2. D
3. C
4. C
5. C
6. D
7. B
8. C
9. B
10. A
11. D
12. A
13. A
14. A
15. B
16. C
17. D
18. D
19. B
20. D

Short-Answer Questions

1. the nominal interest rate minus the expected inflation rate

2. A rise in the real interest rate increases the incentive to save.

3. A rise in the real interest rate reduces the incentive to invest.

4. A government budget deficit exists when government spending exceeds tax revenues.

5. A government budget surplus exists when tax revenues exceed government spending.

6. crowding out

7. Because output is supply determined, if the government consumes more output by operating with a budget deficit, there is less output available for private consumption.

8. A rise in money growth leads to a higher expected inflation rate, which is added to the real interest rate to yield a higher nominal interest rate.

9. by dividing the home nation's price level by the foreign nation's price level

10. a nation that whose residents exchange goods, services, and financial assets with the residents of other nations

Chapter 5

Multiple-Choice Questions

1. C
2. A
3. D
4. A
5. A
6. B
7. D
8. B
9. A
10. C
11. D
12. C
13. B
14. B
15. A
16. C
17. D
18. D
19. B
20. A

Short-Answer Questions

1. an annual rate of growth that accumulates across years

2. aggregate real GDP divided by the nation's population

3. by raising labor supply, equilibrium employment, and equilibrium aggregate output with an unchanged population

4. supply-side economists

5. Gross investment includes depreciation, while net investment excludes depreciation.

6. immigration

7. an increase in the marginal productivity of labor or capital

8. net investment

9. human capital

10. a quota

Chapter 6

Multiple-Choice Questions

1. B
2. A
3. B
4. D
5. A
6. A
7. C
8. C
9. A
10. B
11. D
12. D
13. A
14. D
15. C
16. D
17. C
18. D
19. B
20. B

Short-Answer Questions

1. a business cycle

2. a depression

3. the percentage of the civilian labor force that is unemployed but seeking work

4. income redistributions managed by the government

5. the level of import spending divided by real disposable income

6. the amount of household consumption spending not related to the level of disposable income

7. the incomes of nations whose residents purchase the exports and the exchange rate

8. Real income is, by definition, equal to the sum of real consumption spending, real realized investment spending, real government expenditures, and real exports.

9. It results from attainment of an equilibrium real income level that is above the long-run, potential level of real income.

10. a decline in the equilibrium balance of trade

Chapter 7

Multiple-Choice Questions

1. D
2. D
3. D
4. A
5. C
6. A
7. A
8. A
9. C
10. B
11. D
12. B
13. C
14. B
15. C
16. C
17. D
18. C
19. C
20. D

Short-Answer Questions

1. income taxes

2. the additional income taxes an individual pays on an additional dollar of income

3. total income taxes divided by total income

4. a tax system in which those with higher total incomes pay a higher percentage of their incomes as income taxes

5. a tax system in which those with higher total incomes pay a lower percentage of their incomes as income taxes

6. If real income declines, so do income taxes, thereby stimulating consumption and pushing equilibrium real income back up somewhat.

7. a schedule indicating that income tax revenues rise as the income tax rate increases above zero percent but ultimately must decline as the income tax rate approaches one-hundred percent

8. a sum that an individual designates for transfer to another person following his or her death

9. a gift or bequest from a member of one age group to someone who is part of a different age group

10. the idea that a tax cut that creates or adds to a deficit induces individuals to save the proceeds of the tax reduction in anticipation of a future tax increase, so that the tax cut does not affect current consumption

Chapter 8

Multiple-Choice Questions

1. B
2. B
3. C
4. A
5. D
6. D
7. C
8. C
9. A
10. A
11. C
12. C
13. B
14. D
15. D
16. A
17. A
18. A
19. B
20. D

Short-Answer Questions

1. a perpetuity

2. a set of combinations of real income and the nominal interest rate for which the market for real money balances is in equilibrium, given the current real stock of money

3. the proportionate change in desired real money balances owing to a proportionate change in the interest rate

4. a set of combinations of real income and the nominal interest rate for which real income equals aggregate desired expenditures, given the current level of aggregate net autonomous expenditures

5. the proportionate change in desired investment owing to a proportionate change in the interest rate

6. a rise (reduction) in the nominal interest rate caused by an increase (decline) in the price level that reduces (raises) the supply of real money balances, given an unchanged nominal quantity of money

7. a rise (reduction) in the nominal interest rate caused by a decline (increase) in the nominal quantity of money that reduces (raises) the supply of real money balances, given an unchanged price level

8. A change in the nominal money stock induces a change in the nominal interest rate, which in turn influences investment, thereby altering equilibrium real income through the Keynesian multiplier effect.

9. when the demand for money is completely interest elastic (so that the *LM* schedule is perfectly elastic) and desired investment is completely interest inelastic (so that the *IS* schedule is perfectly inelastic)

10. when the demand for money is completely interest inelastic (so that the *LM* schedule is perfectly inelastic) and desired investment is completely interest elastic (so that the *IS* schedule is perfectly elastic)

Chapter 9

Multiple-Choice Questions

1. D   5. D   9. A   13. B   17. C
2. A   6. A   10. B   14. A   18. D
3. C   7. A   11. B   15. A   19. C
4. B   8. C   12. B   16. C   20. D

Short-Answer Questions

1. Internal balance refers to attainment of a target value for a domestic variable, such as real income.

2. External balance refers to attainment of a target value of private international payment flows.

3. a set of combinations of real income and the nominal interest rate consistent with attainment of a particular value, such as zero, for the private payments balance

4. the degree to which financial resources can flow across a nation's borders

5. legal restrictions on flows of financial resources across a nation's borders

6. A relatively higher degree of capital mobility makes the *BP* schedule relatively more shallow.

7. A depreciation of the domestic currency causes the *BP* schedule to shift rightward.

8. an action to keep changes in foreign exchange reserves from altering the total quantity of money in circulation

9. A monetary expansion pushes down the domestic interest rate, which creates a private payments deficit that places downward pressure on the value of the nation's currency. Keeping the exchange rate fixed requires selling foreign exchange reserves, and this reduces the money stock once again, thereby bringing about a reversal of the effects of the monetary policy action.

10. An expansionary fiscal policy pushes up the domestic interest rate, which in the case of relatively high capital mobility creates a private payments surplus that places upward pressure on the value of the nation's currency. Keeping the exchange rate fixed requires buying foreign exchange reserves, and this raises the money stock, thereby reinforcing the real income effect of the fiscal policy action.

Chapter 10

Multiple-Choice Questions

1. C
2. C
3. D
4. A
5. D
6. D
7. B
8. A
9. D
10. C
11. B
12. A
13. A
14. B
15. A
16. B
17. C
18. D
19. B
20. C

Short-Answer Questions

1. Each price level-real income combination implies an *IS-LM* equilibrium.

2. an implicit contract

3. the demand for labor by firms, or the value of labor's marginal product

4. sticky or inflexible nominal wages or imperfect information about the price level

5. if the aggregate supply schedule slopes upward or, equivalently, if the Phillips curve slopes downward

6. a period short enough that expected inflation is not equal to actual inflation

7. a period short enough that expected inflation is equal to actual inflation

8. the natural rate of unemployment

9. It is fixed.

10. It is equal to the actual inflation rate.

Chapter 11

Multiple-Choice Questions

1. A	5. C	9. A	13. B	17. B
2. D	6. A	10. C	14. A	18. C
3. C	7. D	11. C	15. D	19. D
4. B	8. B	12. A	16. D	20. B

Short-Answer Questions

1. an expectation based solely on past information

2. an expectation based on past and current information and on an understanding of the workings of the economy

3. the claim that systematic, predictable monetary and fiscal policy actions cannot influence real output or employment

4. a model in which each individual consumer, worker, or firm has the same information and the same conception of how the economy functions

5. Fed watching

6. The market is inefficient.

7. The rate of exchange of a nation's currency for an amount of foreign currency to be delivered at a future date.

8. covered interest parity

9. uncovered interest parity

10. The forward premium equals anticipated depreciation plus a risk premium.

Chapter 12

Multiple-Choice Questions

1. A
2. B
3. C
4. D
5. A
6. B
7. C
8. D
9. B
10. B
11. D
12. C
13. A
14. C
15. C
16. A
17. C
18. A
19. B
20. D

Short-Answer Questions

1. This term refers to the fact that the essential new classical and modern Keynesian contracting theories both make the same basic prediction, that an unanticipated rise in the price level leads to a short-term expansion of real output.

2. cost-of-living-adjustment (COLA) contracts

3. a tendency for the aggregate real wage to rise during intervals in which real output rises due to increased aggregate demand

4. a tendency for the aggregate real wage to fall during intervals in which real output rises due to increased aggregate demand

5. the expected nominal wage that would have been determined by labor-market equilibrium in the absence of a contract

6. contracts with the same beginning and ending dates

7. contracts whose beginning and ending dates and/or durations do not coincide

8. It causes the optimal term of the contract to decline.

9. It causes the optimal term of the contract to increase.

10. a macroeconomic model in which some sectors of the economy have wage contracts but others do not

Chapter 13

Multiple-Choice Questions

1.	B	5.	D	9.	C	13.	D	17.	B
2.	C	6.	B	10.	D	14.	B	18.	C
3.	C	7.	D	11.	B	15.	B	19.	A
4.	A	8.	A	12.	D	16.	A	20.	C

Short-Answer Questions

1. observations of economic variables that span relatively long intervals

2. a tendency for the price level to resist change over time

3. a failure of a private market equilibrium to reflect all costs and benefits relating to production of a good or service

4. a spillover effect that arises when market transactions influence the well-being of an individual or firm not involved in the market

5. a situation in which equilibrium in most markets fails to account for spillovers across the markets, so that equilibrium macroeconomic variables differ from their long-run, natural levels.

6. a hypothesis that imperfectly competitive firms that can keep prices relatively inflexible over lengthy periods

7. the inability of workers and firms to plan and implement labor supply, production, and pricing decisions because of macroeconomic externalities that affect workers and firms differently

8. an interdependence of the economic decisions that people make individually or as part of groups

9. currency and bank reserves that a central bank can control

10. calibration

Chapter 14

Multiple-Choice Questions

1.	A	5.	D	9.	A	13.	C	17.	B
2.	B	6.	D	10.	C	14.	C	18.	A
3.	A	7.	C	11.	A	15.	B	19.	D
4.	D	8.	C	12.	D	16.	C	20.	B

Short-Answer Questions

1. the Humphrey-Hawkins Act of 1978

2. zero inflation; 3 percent unemployment

3. the Employment Act of 1946

4. the interest rate that the Federal Reserve charges on loans to private banks

5. Federal Reserve purchases or sales of government securities

6. a macroeconomic variable that a central bank such as the Federal Reserve aims to achieve in the hope of attaining its ultimate objectives

7. the total accumulation of all amounts owed to private owners of government securities issued from the past through the present

8. An increase in the government budget deficit crowds out private investment spending, which reduces growth of the capital stock and thereby contributes to lower economic growth.

9. If the government allocates surplus funds less efficiently than the private sector, then on net it contributes less to economic growth than private investors would have contributed.

10. whether to assign internal balance or external balance objectives to the government or to the central bank

Chapter 15

Multiple-Choice Questions

1. D
2. C
3. A
4. D
5. B
6. D
7. A
8. A
9. B
10. C
11. C
12. B
13. C
14. D
15. A
16. B
17. A
18. C
19. B
20. C

Short-Answer Questions

1. the recognition lag

2. the response lag

3. the transmission lag

4. roughly one year

5. discretionary monetary policy

6. the output level that an economy could produce if all its resources were employed to their utmost capability

7. that policymakers act in the best interest of society as a whole

8. that policymakers act in their own best interest

9. a central banker contract

10. a monetary policymaker that must issue local currency that is 100 percent backed by the currency of another nation

Chapter 16

Multiple-Choice Questions

1. B
2. D
3. C
4. D
5. A
6. B
7. A
8. C
9. C
10. D
11. A
12. C
13. D
14. B
15. A
16. D
17. C
18. D
19. C
20. C

Short-Answer Questions

1. the possibility that unexpected changes in asset market values can occur as a result of changes in the value of a nation's currency

2. a strategy aimed at offsetting the risk arising from variations in exchange rates

3. a region within which exchange rates could be fixed without slowing adjustments of employment and output to altered conditions in geographic areas within the region

4. international economic integration

5. Perfect capital mobility is a situation in which financial resources are as mobile across a nation's borders as they are inside its borders.

6. Under perfect capital mobility, international interest parity conditions (covered and uncovered interest parities) are satisfied, so that in the absence of anticipated exchange rate changes the domestic interest rate will equal the foreign interest rate; alternatively stated, even the smallest change in the domestic interest rate will induce very large swings in capital flows leading to an immediate return to private payments balance with the domestic interest rate at parity with the foreign interest rate.

7. Dollarization is a general term for a nation's use of another country's currency as the medium of exchange, unit of account, store of value, and standard of deferred payment within its own borders.

8. Portfolio investment involves the purchase of less than 10 percent of the assets of a foreign firm, whereas foreign direct investment involves buying more than 10 percent of the firm's assets.

Chapter 16 (continued)

9. One view is that international financial crises arise from a mismatch of the nation's exchange rate with the rate of exchange consistent with economic fundamentals that will determine its value. The second perspective is that all that is required is for traders to develop a perception that policymakers' commitments to current exchange rates are not credible, so that self-fulfilling anticipations will create major swings in currency values. The third view emphasizes the role of government policies that create moral hazard problems in financial markets that give borrowers an incentive to misuse funds they obtain from lenders.

10. The basic goal of an early warning system is to predict international financial crises before they occur, so that policymakers can engage in policies designed to prevent them from occurring or to limit the severity of the crises.

Notes